THE
GOD
MYTH
AND
OTHER
LIES

HEATHER THOMPSON DAY

THE GOD MYTH AND OTHER LIES

REVIEW AND HERALD® PUBLISHING ASSOCIATION

Since 1861 | www.reviewandherald.com

Published by Review and Herald® Publishing Association, Hagerstown, MD 21741-1119

This book was
Edited by JoAlyce Waugh
Copyedited by Tom Fraga
Cover design by Daniel Anéz
Cover art by Copyright © Thinkstock
Typeset: 11/13 Minion Pro

PRINTED IN U.S.A.

18 17 16 15 14   5 4 3 2 1

Library of Congress Cataloging-in-Publication Data
Day, Heather Thompson.
  The god myth and other lies / Heather Thompson Day.
    pages cm
  ISBN 978-0-8280-2716-8
  1. Apologetics. I. Title.
  BT1103.D395 2014
  239--dc23
                              2013002962
ISBN 978-0-8280-2716-8

I dedicate this book

to my loving friends (you know who you are)—
Christian, atheist, and agnostic.

It has been through thought-provoking conversations with you that I've not only figured out exactly what I believe but done the research so I know why. You've supported me, pushed me, and caused me to think. For that I am eternally grateful. May all the roads we travel lead us to the same destination: heaven.

With love,
Heather Marie

Contents

Dear Reader,

This is a book that puts researchable knowledge into everyday language while attempting to provide you with answers to underlying seeds of doubt that may be germinating. Do I believe in God just because it "feels good"? *The God Myth and Other Lies* provides firm confidence to bolster what could be shaky faith.

Sixty percent of young people are leaving the church.* This is a statistic I feel obligated to help change, which is why I wrote this book. I am an instructor at a secular community college, and I have been overwhelmed by the conversations I've overheard among my students regarding their belief systems. I believe college is where 6 out of 10 young people lose their belief in God. Suddenly they are in a new environment with a new sense of freedom, and if they have selected a secular campus, they will, without a doubt, experience an assault on their faith. Sadly, I think the average Christian is simply ill-prepared for what they will encounter. I have actually lost sleep over this statistic, and I want to provide high school seniors and college students with answers that will strengthen their faith.

After listening to classroom banter, which centers on personal belief systems more often than you may think, I have been convicted of one thing: the average young adult Christian doesn't really know why they believe in God, other than their parents told them to. When they meet professors and students who know exactly why they *don't* believe in God, and often with bibliographic reasons, these young Christians get confused. God has given us many reasons to be confident in His existence, and unfortunately the average Christian young person doesn't have a clue how much proof exists. I know God is real, and my background in academia has forced me to want to find facts for my faith. I want to share what I've learned because knowledge is contagious, and in these last days God is going to need young people who are confident in Him.

This truly is war! Are you prepared for the battle?

---

*www.christianitytoday.com/le/2012/winter/youngleavechurch.html.

Chapter 1

Aliens May Have Created Life on Earth

"It isn't a question of whether or not flying saucers exist. The question is What are they and whom do they belong to?"
—George Filer, U.S. Air Force intelligence officer, 1958-1978[1]

The reason I decided I needed to write this book is a study I read by the Barna Group, one of the leading research organizations in the country that focuses on faith and culture. The study was about the disconnect between young people and the church. Their findings suggested that nearly three out of every five young people disconnect from the church after the age of 15. The Christian church is losing nearly 60 percent of its youth every year. One of the reasons cited for this disconnect is the gap between Christianity and science.[2] I am a communications instructor at a secular college. While watching and listening to young people as they come and go from their classrooms, I have observed that if a Christian wishes to attend a non-Christian college, it is important that their faith be rock-solid. Unfortunately, that is a lot to ask. The average Christian doesn't study or research why others don't believe God exists; they are simply taught that He does, and not to question it.

Regrettably, they are then thrown into classrooms in which they meet charismatic, highly intelligent, and very successful professors who counter their belief in God, and not just with opinions, but with loads of research they present as proof. Religion in a secular school is taught as a philosophy. It is not scientific, and therefore is simply thrown in with all the other philosophical ideas people may choose to embrace, such as Greek mythology, Hinduism, and Buddhism. When Christ-believing, churchgoing students object to something in their professors' lectures and try to voice their concerns, they often find that faith doesn't get them very far when they're arguing against someone with credible research and knowledge that suddenly seems so much larger than their "feelings."

My husband took a college philosophy class in which the teacher asked the students to raise their hands if they believed in Jesus. A few shaky hands went up, the students unsure if they wanted to identify themselves since they didn't know where the teacher would be going with this.

His next question to them was: "Why do you believe in Jesus?"

One student responded by sharing his faith testimony. We have all heard similar stories before: he was going through a tough time, life was terrible, he had a bad family, and suddenly Jesus stepped in and he has never been the same.

The professor smiled and said, "What if I was to tell you that your belief in Jesus, rather than an actual Jesus, is what made all the difference? Belief is powerful. Whether it is Bigfoot, the tooth fairy, or Zeus, a person's belief can help better their situation. If you had held just as tight to the belief that Bigfoot was watching over you, that ideology would have been just as beneficial."

He then turned to the rest of the class and said, "Belief in God, not God, is what Christians cling to. It's simply having a belief. There is no God, but belief is powerful." My husband had attended church schools his entire life, and he was shocked at the brazen disrespect for the man who had just given his testimony and the disrespect toward Christ that this professor had just shown. When he came home and told me the story, I was not at all surprised. I have heard this argument time and again.

My husband also said that by the end of the semester, he overheard some students talking among themselves about their belief in God. "I don't really know what I believe anymore," one girl said.

And in my opinion, this is where our youth are going. They are unprepared for the never-ending assault the world will be bringing on their faith. If you have always surrounded yourself with believers, it could be quite confusing to suddenly meet unbelievers—and unbelievers who are educated and have thought-provoking reasons for their disbelief. But here's the secret the devil is hoping you will never know: it doesn't have to!

It may shock naive Christian youth to learn that there are quite a few people out there who dislike Christianity and everything it represents. I've noticed that many professors would prefer that you be Buddhist or Hindu than believe that Jesus Christ is Lord. I am not sure what it is about Christianity that puts such a sour taste in the mouth of academia, but it is an issue that youth attending these schools need to be prepared to deal with.

How do you know you believe in God? How do you know He is not just a myth created thousands of years ago by men who were high on opiates? (This is an argument I am citing from a colleague's lecture.) I think it is important for every Christian to do some soul searching, whether attending a private or a secular school. We all need to figure out not just what we believe, but why. We will indeed encounter many people in our lives who will make it their duty to destroy our faith. If we don't start evaluating why we believe or practice these things, we will not stand a chance when we discuss it with others who know exactly why they don't believe. If a seed of faith can move mountains, what can a seed of doubt destroy?

I sat in on a colleague's lecture not long ago and listened to him explain religion as a philosophy to his humanities students.

"How do you know aliens did not start life here on earth? There is plenty of research and comments from NASA executives and past presidents that would propose that aliens are real. If they are real, how do we know that they did not get things started for us on this planet? How can you be sure they didn't, if you were not there?"

"How do we know?" was the general sentiment of the students, some of whom probably entered the room believing Christ was the originator of life. They then discussed the possibility of truth existing in other religions besides Christianity. Christianity, after all, is not the oldest religion; generally we consider Hinduism the oldest religion. Wouldn't the most truth be found in the first religion?

Penn Jillette wrote an essay for NPR's *This I Believe* segment. The title of his essay was "There Is No God." He ends his thoughts with this:

"Believing there is no God means the suffering I've seen in my family, and indeed all the suffering in the world, isn't caused by an omniscient, omnipresent, omnipotent force that isn't bothered to help or is just testing us, but rather something we all may be able to help others with in the future. No God means the possibility of less suffering in the future.

"Believing there is no God gives me more room for belief in family, people, love, truth, beauty, sex, Jell-O and all the other things I can prove and that make this life the best life I will ever have." [3]

Here he sums up one of the biggest arguments critics bring to Christianity: if there is a God, why is there suffering?

Andrew Zak Williams put together an article called "Faith No More." [4] In it he compiled reasons given by many different atheists why they don't believe in God. Below are excerpts of some of the reasons three individuals gave. I want you to see them as a framework for what you can expect to encounter if you choose to attend a secular college or even work in a non-church- affiliated organization. Anytime you step foot outside your church pew, you may readily be in contact with antagonists of Christ. And in my opinion, before you can answer the question of why you believe what you believe, you should always be able to look at the other arguments. Why don't they believe? Are their opinions credible?

Maryam Namazie, a human rights activist, writes:

"I suppose people can go through an entire lifetime without questioning God and a religion that they were born into (out of no choice of their own), especially if it doesn't have much of a say in their lives. If you live in France or Britain, there may never be a need to renounce God actively or come out as an atheist.

"But when the state sends a 'Hezbollah' [the generic term for Islamist] to your school to ensure that you don't mix with your friends who are boys, stops you from swimming, forces you to be veiled, deems males and females separate and unequal, prescribes different books for you and your girlfriends from those read by boys, denies certain fields of study to you because you are female, and starts killing indiscriminately, then you have no choice but to question, discredit and confront it—all of it. And that is what I did."

Kenan Malik, a neurobiologist, writer, and broadcaster, explained his views this way:

"I am an atheist because I see no need for God. . . .

"Invoking God at best highlights what we cannot yet explain about the physical universe, and at worst exploits that ignorance to mystify. Moral values do not come prepackaged from God, but have to be worked out by human beings through a combination of empathy, reasoning and dialogue. . . .

"And it is not God that gives meaning to our lives, but our relationships with fellow human beings and the goals and obligations that derive from them. God is at best redundant, at worst an obstruction. Why do I need him?"

Susan Blackmore, a psychologist and author, writes:

"What reason for belief could I possibly have? To explain suffering? He doesn't. Unless, that is, you buy in to his giving us free will, which conflicts with all we know about human decision-making.

"To give me hope of an afterlife? My 30 years of parapsychological research threw that hope out. To explain the mystical, spiritual and out-of-body experiences I have had? No: our rapidly improving knowledge of the brain is providing much better explanations than religious reasoning. To explain the existence and complexity of the wonderful world I see around me? No—and this is really the main one.

"God is supposed (at least in some versions of the story) to have created us all. Yet the Creator (any creator) is simply redundant. Every living thing on this planet evolved by processes that require no designer, no plans, no guidance and no foresight. We need no God to do this work. Where would he fit in? What would he do? And why? If he did have any role in our creation, he would have to be immensely devious, finickity, deceitful and mind-bogglingly cruel, which would be a very odd kind of God to believe in. So I don't."

I want you to see these arguments so that you are not completely thrown off kilter when you interact with people who spout similar ideas. Every semester—just yesterday, in fact—I have had a student in my classroom explaining why he or she didn't believe in God. "I believe in science. I believe in truth I can prove," they say.

The uneducated Christian may begin to doubt his or her own beliefs when faced with such well-constructed criticism. *Is there really no proof for God? Is my belief system all about faith with zero facts?* I hope this book will build up shaky faith. Facts improve faith, and what you may not have known before you opened this book is that the case for God likely contains more facts than any other idea in the world. In fact, there is quite possibly no greater truth than the truth that God exists and is in control. I hope to equip you with an arsenal of proof that will add conviction and confidence to your faith. God is good, and He doesn't want you to be deceived.

I believe the worldview of theism has had a considerable impact on education. There is a great move in education, perhaps because of too much theism in America's history, to do away with theistic logic altogether. General education has moved so far away from theism that it is forced to respond to theism by rejecting it. Theism asserts that God is the originator and creator of life and the universe. Educators respond by spending much time researching all sorts of other plausible modes of existence. Buddhists, Hindus, scientists, and so on try to provide us with other avenues of creation. Postmodernism replies by asking, "Who is to say for certain which one has truth?"

In the world's eyes, you are open-minded if you are agnostic, you may be scientific if you are atheist, and you are well-traveled and philosophical if you are Buddhist. But if you are Christian, you are a fool. In the Bible the Israelites dealt with the issue of pagan gods. Today we are dealing with the same mysticism in a different form. Satan has disguised science as a god, and Eastern religions as open-minded, beautiful philosophies that can enhance the soul. Satan is still providing the world with false gods today, just as he did in the Old Testament era. Satan is always busy, and he is a brilliant, strategic opponent. How in the world can you face him?

You don't stand a chance alone. But by spending each day with Christ, saturating yourself in His Word, and talking with Him in prayer, you will be enlightened. The Bible is absolutely incredible, and the average Christian doesn't even realize how much artistry was crafted in those pages. You need to know why you believe what you believe, because if you don't you're easy prey for Satan, who is working tirelessly to destroy you.

I cannot stress to you enough the importance of including the study of the Scriptures into your daily life. The Bible is truly remarkable, and Christ orchestrated its creation in such a way that if there were never another devotional, prayer, or spiritual book written, the Bible would be enough to save our souls. Christ spent a great deal of energy in making sure His disciples understood that they must love the Word of God in order to truly know the Father.

Matthew 4:4 says, "But Jesus told him, 'No! The Scriptures say, "People do not live by bread alone, but by every word that comes from the mouth of God"'" (NLT).

Christ says that we shouldn't just read Scripture—we must feed on it. It must be what sustains us, and holds all things together.

John 8:31, 32 says, "Jesus then said to the Jews who had believed in him, "If you continue in my word, you are truly my disciples, and you will know the truth, and the truth will make you free" (RSV).

The Bible is what will set us free. Books such as this one that you are reading are great and necessary, but please, make no mistake, it is the Bible that will free you, enlighten you, and transform your mind and heart. This book, without that book, means nothing.

Joshua 1:8 says, "Keep this Book of the Law always on your lips; meditate on it day and night, so that you may be careful to do everything written in it. Then you will be prospersous and successful."

We need to understand the Word of God in order to be successful. Do not underestimate its power.

And last, my favorite verse in reference to Scripture, John 14:23, 24, "Jesus answered and said to him, 'If anyone loves Me, he will keep My word; and My Father will love him, and We will come to him and We will come to him and make Our home with him. He who does not love Me does not keep My words; and the word which you hear is not Mine but the Father's who sent Me'" (NKJV).

Christ goes so far as to say that if you love Him, you must love His Word. Satan is hoping that you will overlook that part. You see, Satan knows how powerful Scripture is. He watched helpless as it sustained Christ in one of His weakest earthly moments while being tempted. Studying Scripture earlier kept Him focused and undeterred while Satan tried all the tricks up his sleeve. Because Christ knew the Father, because the Father lived in Him, Satan's offerings were petty, because everything seems small in comparison to a God so big. Study the Word of God. It will strengthen your faith, enlighten your mind, and secure your heart. That book stands alone, and never let anyone tell you different.

Back to that lecture I recently sat in on by a colleague who just happened to be discussing religion as a philosophy during a humanities class. He was explaining to the students that the theists' need for a God is simply the human need to seek something bigger than ourselves when we are in some kind of trouble. We live an agnostic or atheistic life, and suddenly, when confronted with death or tragedy, we seek out help, and that help comes in the form of a god. Science says that all truth must be provable, and how can education, which teaches science, also teach God?

And this is when I heard my all-time favorite explanation for the creation of life while sitting mutely in his classroom, just listening and gauging the reactions of these impressionable young people to his words. Again with the aliens! I was particularly intrigued with his explanation that the idea of alien life forms traveling to earth and implanting life here was just as plausible as Christians believing God created the heavens and earth. His point was that since we were not here to witness our creation, it's just as likely that aliens could have been responsible for our existence as God.

Now, if some guy on a street corner told these exact same students the exact same thing—that aliens might have created life on earth—they would have laughed. They would have kept walking, blown it off, and maybe retold the story as a joke. However, when their professor, whom they already deem as credible because of his intelligence, education, and extremely charismatic speaking style, tells them that aliens may have created life on earth, they shut up and they listen.

Many of those students who entered that classroom that day as lukewarm Christians walked out with doubts. I could hear them whisper to one another, "I'm not sure what I really believe anymore."

That is when I knew this was a serious problem, and I had to address it. You see, the average Christian is taught that God is real, but no one really says why. A professor in the Theological Seminary at Andrews University, Allan Walshe, maintains that Christians shouldn't waste time arguing over whether postmodernism is good or bad; instead, they should recognize that it exists and figure out how to respond to it.

So where does this leave us? How do we, as Christians, reply to this criticism of a Lord we love so deeply, of a faith we believe in? How do we respond? Do we answer logic with explanations about our feelings? I don't think that is always appropriate. I think it is time we answer logic with logic. We should be able to explain why we believe in God through logic because God is logical. In fact, the idea that He exists is even logical. Just because some individuals with a few degrees and a podium tell you that God is ridiculous doesn't mean that you are wrong. One day those same professors are going to bow their knee and confess that God is God. Their logic and their degrees won't help them, and their charisma won't save them.

This is the first point I want you to internalize: Don't be swayed by human beings, because as Jesus said in Matthew 5:36, "you cannot make even one hair white or black."

The biggest lesson I have learned in life is not to feel afraid to question other people's ideas simply because they sound convincing when they say them. It is my hope that Christians will start preparing themselves for these types of conversations. Don't underestimate the power or genius of the devil. It is our responsibility as ambassadors for Christ to start answering these questions logically. Take heart—God is real! God is present! God has the answers! Let us start studying Him prayerfully and logically, so that we can share what we learn with others.

I do not and will not pretend to have all the answers. There is a certain level of faith that must exist when believing in Christ, but there is also logical research available. I will share what I have studied with you, and I hope it helps assure your heart that you are on the right track. Your faith and beliefs are not silly. Don't be shaken by critics who want to make you uncertain of your ideas. Don't be threatened just because someone who is wearing a nice suit and who possesses a big vocabulary tells you you're wrong.

Yes, the devil is an impressive adversary, but it was Christ who walked these streets and was called Teacher. It was Christ who was called when someone needed to be healed, although He had no degree in medicine. It was Christ who was called King and Lord, although He had no earthly throne or scepter. Even when Jewish rulers tried to destroy Him, the grave could not contain His glory. Christ tells us in John 16:33, "I have told you these things, so that in me you may have peace. In this world you will have trouble. But take heart! I have overcome the world."

So what would I say if faced with the claim that aliens created life on earth? I firmly believe that Jesus is the key for Christians when they are trying to explain the logic for their faith. And once we believe in Jesus, we can take heart in the words He has given us, much like the message He shared with the disciples in the sixteenth chapter of John. You see, He has already claimed the victory, and if you are going to pick a team, you might want to ally yourself with the one that wins.

I grew up a Christian. My parents told me about God daily, and yet as a child I had small moments of doubt when I wasn't sure He existed.

When I was about 6 years old, I never slept without my night-light. It was a rustic-looking night-light with a brown base and pink shade covering a fragile white bulb. The light it radiated was pink and made me feel like a princess as I lay on my lilac sheets.

My favorite color was actually pink. But my mother found a complete bedding set consisting of a lilac bedspread with matching comforter, sheets, and pillowcases on sale at the discount store. And just like that, my identity switched. My favorite color had to be lilac. At least that's what I told any friends who entered my room.

Family members, who never asked me what my favorite color was, started sending me lilac-colored gifts every Christmas and birthday because of that comforter. And so that little pink night-light shade became my fortress. Of all my possessions, it was the only thing in my entire room that I thought represented who I was.

In a way it was that night-light that crippled me and the reason I questioned my belief in God: I was afraid of the dark. Something about a world I couldn't see terrified me. I'd hold my hand in front of my face to calm my nerves. As long as my eyes adjusted enough to see my hand, I knew I was still a person. I was so afraid of the dark that I took up reading. I didn't really like reading yet, but it was about the only reason my mother would permit me to keep my night-light on for another hour.

So I started getting these little paperback children's books with the big pictures and the words that rhymed, the ones in which the entire plot consisted of Johnny going to and from the store to buy eggs. Anything that would keep a fence between the night and me. Reading also made me tired because I found it so boring. Usually after a few chapters Johnny would buy one carton of eggs and meet Jane at the park, and then I would fall asleep almost instantly and never feel the angst of tossing and turning without the pink light.

I rationalized in my 6-year-old brain that if I believed in God I wouldn't be afraid of anything. If I truly felt His presence, the night wouldn't even faze me. But since I was scared, I took that to mean that I doubted Him. It's not so ludicrous, really. It is true that we have nothing to fear with Christ beside us. I think of Him as the front line on the battlefield. Except since He never loses, I never have to fight. Not a real fight, anyway. More like the kind of fights you have with your brothers and sisters when you know your parents are in the next room. You have to worry only so much about how hard they'll hit you before your mother makes them regret it.

One night, however, I found out exactly what I did believe. The bulb in my night-light blew in the middle of page 12. I held my breath for as long as I could before I passed out. I bit my lip and squished my entire body into a ball so small that it seemed to fit underneath my pillow. I was debating whether or not I should go to my mom's room and confess to her that all my reading was because of my fear of darkness rather than my newfound intelligence.

I decided I couldn't. I just had to make it through the night, and tomorrow my daddy would replace the bulb and all would be right with the world. I started to cry as I hid from my room. You can't hide from darkness, though. It creeps into all the places you don't want it to. I prayed a few prayers that I had learned from church while I rocked my body back and forth beneath that pillow.

And then it happened—the very first miracle I witnessed, and I watched it from right between my sheets. Almost as subtly as I flipped the pages in my books, the lightbulb flickered and then stayed on. I stared at it for at least 20 minutes, seemingly without blinking. I watched the pink beams dance on my walls and smiled because I knew God existed.

And then I thought maybe it wasn't that I was afraid of the dark because I didn't believe in God; maybe I was afraid of the dark so that one day I could see Him for myself. It was only when I was completely outside of my comfort zone that He first spoke to me. Looking back, I am reminded how God really does care about everything, even 6-year-olds who are afraid of darkness.

When I woke up the next morning, the lightbulb was dead. To this day I've never shared that story with anyone. I guess I thought of it the same way I think of wishes: if you tell someone your wish, it doesn't come true, or rather, it didn't actually happen. My lamp was a secret between God and me. He spoke to me that night as I lay scrunched up underneath my pillow. It's ironic, too, because when I think of it now, I still think of that incident as one of my defining arguments for proof that God exists. All of my research pales in comparison to this one moment when I was 6 years old and I felt as though He heard me. I know it may sound silly, which is why I've never voiced it. But that light was important to me that day.

Shortly afterward I stopped sleeping with my night-light on. From time to time I still used it to read, and I cherished it a little more than I had before—and not just because it was pink. It just looked bigger to me now and more defined. It shined brighter. I wasn't scared of the dark after that ordeal, either. I didn't have to be. There's no need to be scared of the dark when you know who the Light is. I had met with God from under my pillow that night, and just to make sure I recognized Him, He was wearing pink.

I share this story with you because I want you to know that within these pages I have compiled a lot of researchable evidence that Christ is real, that Jesus walked this earth, and that you can rest easy knowing through academic material that God is not a myth. Still, in spite of what we discover together, hold on to your personal moments of faith. Hold on to whatever it is God has done for you that spoke to you personally. He isn't always as conventional as textbooks, but He gets the job done. You can know that there is factual research proving God is and was who He said He was and is. But please, hold on to your night-light moments—they are yours forever, secrets between God and you that no one else may ever believe. But then again, you probably don't need them to.

Response to Critic Number One

Claim: Aliens created life on earth.

Reply: First, can you explain to me why it is easier for you to accept the idea that aliens created life on earth than the idea that God, another intelligent designer, created life? Both of these ideas require intelligent design. If, for whatever reason, you are committed to the notion that aliens created life on earth, you have to eventually respond to the question "Who made the aliens?" At this point you would either have to continue acknowledging a series of alien interventions or eventually say that God did. If, by chance, you responded that aliens were created by evolution, you'd have to explain why you didn't just say evolution instead of aliens.

---

[1] www.gufon.no/agenda/quotes.htm.

[2] www.christianitytoday.com/le/2012/winter/youngleavechurch.html.

[3] Penn Jillette, "There Is No God," This I Believe, National Public Radio, Nov. 21, 2005.

[4] Andrew Zak Williams, "Faith No More," *New Statesman*, July 25, 2011.

Chapter 2

Jesus Christ:
Nice Guy, but Certainly Not Lord

"The reality is that Judaism doesn't regard Jesus as particularly important. He's not a big subject."
—David Klinghoffer, Jewish author[1]

Fact: Jesus existed. We have historical documents proving this, so this issue is not up for discussion. In fact, I remember reading about Jesus in my public high school history book. The fact that Jesus lived and was a leader with followers is not up for debate even in most Darwinian rhetoric. I will note that there is a small group of scholars who do question whether or not He truly existed, but the consensus with most historians is that He did. The question is not whether Jesus was a real person but rather was He who He said He was, and how can we be sure?

To Jews, Jesus is a nonissue. Some may regard Him as simply a failed messiah attempt, and others as a great leader and good man. To Muslims, Jesus was one of God's important prophets, and even a bringer of scripture, but not Lord. Christians, however, worship Jesus and believe He is a member of the Trinity. He is referred to as the Son of God and is said to have died sacrificially in order that we sinful humans may be saved. Some historians who have studied the life of Jesus believe He was a Jewish leader who taught a charismatic restoration movement that anticipated the end of the world. All agree that Jesus of Galilee was crucified by Pontius Pilate.

The majority of historians believe the writings of Josephus to be genuine since his writings focused not on the Christian message, but on the events of his era. He was a renowned Jewish historian who published several books and was also for a time the governor of Galilee, the region it is said Jesus was from. Josephus mentioned a man he called James, and noted that he was the brother of Jesus:

"And now Caesar, upon hearing the death of Festus, sent Albinus into Judea, as procurator. But the king deprived Joseph of the high priesthood, and bestowed the succession to that dignity on the son of Ananus, who was also himself called Ananus. . . . Festus was now dead, and Albinus was but upon the road; so he assembled the sanhedrim of judges, and brought before them the brother of Jesus, who was called Christ, whose name was James, and some others [or, some of his companions]; and when he had formed an accusation against them as breakers of the law, he delivered them to be stoned." [2]

Josephus also referred to the imprisonment and death of John the Baptist: "Now some of the Jews thought that the destruction of Herod's army came from God, and that very justly, as a punishment of what he did against John, that was called the Baptist: for Herod slew him, who was a good man. . . . Herod, who feared lest the great influence John had over the people might put it into his power and inclination to raise a rebellion, . . . thought it best . . . [to put] him to death. Accordingly he was sent a prisoner, out of Herod's suspicious temper, to Macherus, the castle I before mentioned, and was there put to death." [3]

Much of the research into the historicity of Jesus leads to three Greco-Roman pagan writers who provide us with passages that correlate with the biblical account of Jesus being crucified by Pontius Pilate. The three writers, who were also non-Christians, lived in the late first and second centuries. These men were Pliny the Younger, Tacitus, and Suetonius. Tacitus wrote about "Christus," also known as Christ, while describing Nero's persecution of Christians:

"Nero fastened the guilt [of starting a blaze that burned most of Rome] and inflicted the most exquisite tortures on a class hated for their abominations, called Christians by the populace. Christus, from whom the name had its origin, suffered the extreme penalty during the reign of Tiberius at the hands of one of our procurators, Pontius Pilatus, and a most mischievous superstition, thus checked for the moment, again broke out not only in Judaea, the first source of the evil, but even in Rome, where all things hideous and shameful from every part of the world find their centre and become popular." [4]

The stance of the scholarly world on the existence of Jesus is somewhat divided. Although a few argue that there is not sufficient evidence to claim He existed at all, the majority believe He did exist as a historical figure, but that there is no proof to support the claims that He was supernatural or that He was who He claimed to be.

The 1997 Encyclopedia Britannica included an article titled "The Apostle Paul," and had this to say about the life of the apostle: "The Apostle Paul is an outstanding figure in the history of Christianity. Converted only a few years after the death of Jesus, he became the leading Apostle (missionary) of the new movement and played a decisive part in extending it beyond the limits of Judaism to become a worldwide religion. His surviving letters are the earliest extant Christian writings." The article goes on to mention the view of many scholars on the credibility of Paul's writings: "There are no reliable sources for Paul's life outside the New Testament. The primary source is his own letters. Of these, Romans, I and II Corinthians, and Galatians are indisputably genuine. Most scholars also accept Philippians, I Thessalonians, and Philemon."[5]

I think it is important to ask a couple of questions at this juncture: If scholars accept many of Paul's writings as having been penned from the very hand of Paul, why would it be hard for us to accept that Jesus also existed? If Paul existed and was converted about three or so years after Christ was crucified, and then spent his entire life radically crusading for the cause of this man, Jesus, why wouldn't we assume that Jesus also existed?

Some of the most brilliant men in history believed Jesus existed, such as Albert Einstein and Napoleon Bonaparte. Napoleon, undoubtedly known best as an extremely successful military and political leader during the French Revolution, certainly did not question the existence of Christ: "I know men and I tell you that Jesus Christ is no mere man. Between Him and every other person in the world there is no possible term of comparison. Alexander, Caesar, Charlemagne, and I have founded empires. But on what did we rest the creation of our genius? Upon force. Jesus Christ founded His empire upon love; and at this hour millions of men would die for Him."[6]

If we agree with much of the scholarly literature suggesting that Christ did exist, we are left to deal with the question of whether He was who He claimed to be. C. S. Lewis writes in his book *Mere Christianity*: "A man who was merely a man and said the sort of things Jesus said would not be a great moral teacher. He would either be a lunatic—on the level with the man who says he is a poached egg—or else he would be the Devil of Hell. You must make your choice. Either this man was, and is, the Son of God: or else a madman or something worse. You can shut Him up for a fool, you can spit at Him and kill Him as a demon; or you can fall at His feet and call Him Lord and God. But let us not come with any patronizing nonsense about His being a great human teacher. He has not left that open to us."[7]

Other religions, such as Confucianism, Hinduism, and Buddhism, were founded by mortal men, human beings just like you and me. These religions are composed of human-made ideologies and moral teachings.

If you separated the leaders of these religions from the practices of these religions, the way followers worship and the life disciplines they exercise would not change much. The "goodness" of the person has to do more with the rituals than anything else. But with Christianity it is just the opposite. If you were to separate Christ from Christianity, what would be left?

When C. S. Lewis said that if Jesus were not Christ He would have been a lunatic, he hit the nail on the head. Jesus does not just teach us moral lessons to follow; He says that without Him, we perish. In John 14:6 He says, "I am the way and the truth and the life. No one comes to the Father except through me."

In John 13:13 He says, "You call me 'Teacher' and 'Lord,' and rightly so, for that is what I am."

And in John 12:44-46 Jesus emphatically declares, "Whoever believes in me does not believe in me only, but in the one who sent me. The one who looks at me is seeing the one who sent me. I have come into the world as a light, so that no one who believes in me should stay in darkness."

Christianity claims that without Christ you are in darkness. You can live a good life, you can love people, you can give to those who are poor, but if you do not accept Jesus Christ as Lord and Savior, then you are still fumbling around in a dark cave without a flashlight. Jesus makes this crystal clear in verses 47-50: "If anyone hears my words but does not keep them, I do not judge that person. For I did not come to judge the world, but to save the world. There is a judge for the one who rejects me and does not accept my words; the very words I have spoken will condemn them at the last day. For I did not speak on my own, but the Father who sent me commanded me to say all that I have spoken. I know that his command leads to eternal life. So whatever I say is just what the Father has told me to say."

Christianity without Jesus is like a human being without a beating heart. Christ is the center of Christianity. If you don't mind I'd like to refer you to Luke 23:39-43. It's a story you are surely familiar with. In fact, this is one of those verses in the Bible that most people, no matter the magnitude of their faith, are familiar with. It's the story of Jesus and the two thieves. I want you to look at this story because not only does it give us a better picture of who Christ was, but also we see fulfillment of prophecy.

Luke 23:39 reads: "Then one of the criminals who were hanged blasphemed Him, saying, 'If You are the Christ, save Yourself and us'" (NKJV).

I'd like to pause here for a moment and just look at what is happening here. Jesus has just suffered the greatest emotional turmoil known to humanity that night in Gethsemane, where the sheer agony of the weight of the sins of this world loaded and burdened onto the back of one man caused Him to sweat literal blood. Not only that, but He finds himself in the next 24 hours betrayed and deserted by the disciples that He called friends. Not only this, but He was also beaten within an inch of His life. He has been mocked by onlookers, battered and bruised. I can imagine Him hanging there, catching the gaze of His mother, whose eyes are, I'm sure, swollen and bloodshot at the sight of her dying Son. . . . And as if this isn't enough, Jesus, the King of kings, the Creator of our universe, is now being jeered and mocked by this criminal, this thief, as He hangs on a cross for that same man's very sin. Wow. That's heavy.

As soon as I finish reading through the Bible cover to cover I open it up and read it again. I am in Luke right now and recently came to this story in my morning worship and I couldn't help sobbing as the reality of what Christ did struck me all over again. Jesus—the Lamb who takes away the sin of the world.

With crucifixion, it was not so much the crime that got one crucified, as it was the status of the person. Crucifixion was a means of execution for slaves, noncitizens, and the army. It was humiliating and degrading and was meant to set an example for the consequences of wrongdoing, as were most Roman methods of execution. However, there was no particular list of crimes that would mark one individual as needing to be killed by crucifixion. A citizen who was convicted of a crime, perhaps theft, would be fined and maybe would be forced to work to pay restitution. But a slave convicted of the same thing could be crucified. And so on two beams of wood hangs our Savior, our Lord, humiliated, receiving the death of a slave. Verse 40 continues: "But the other, answering, rebuked him, saying, 'Do you not even fear God, seeing you are under the same condemnation? And we indeed justly, for we receive the due reward of our deeds; but this Man has done nothing wrong.' Then he said to Jesus, 'Lord, remember me when You come into Your kingdom' " (NKJV).

"Remember me, Jesus," He pleads. In this man I see the picture of grace. At the eleventh hour of his life he comes to Christ and asks for forgiveness. He acknowledges his sin, and he asks Jesus to remember him when He enters heaven. Christ could have ignored that man. He did have a lot going on at that moment. He could have rebuked him and said, "Remember you? When did you ever remember Me? Now you come to Me? Now? At the last hours of your life? In the last moments of your breath you seek Me? Where were you when I called you? Why did you not answer all those days and nights I stood knocking at the door of your heart begging you to let Me in?" Christ could have said that, and justly.

But no, Christ's response reminds me of one of my favorite quotes by Mark Lowry. "God spreads grace the way a 5-year-old spreads peanut butter—He gets it all over everything."

Jesus responds in verse 43, "And Jesus said to him, 'Assuredly, I say to you, today you will be with Me in Paradise'" (NKJV).

What a story! Jesus Christ still saving souls on the last leg of His earthly ministry. Jesus, still worried about the fate of His children, though they have pierced Him and hung Him to a tree. "*Eli Eli lama sabachthani?*" (Matthew 27:46, NKJV) He cried that day. "My God, my God, why have You forsaken Me?"

In the crying out in this verse Jesus, though dying, is still preaching. He is quoting Psalm 22:1, which also says: "My God, My God, why have You forsaken Me?" He is quoting arguably the most influential patriarch in Jewish history, King David. You see, nearly 1,000 years before, in Psalm 22, David cited this method of excruciating death that would be suffered by the coming Messiah. In the 1,000 years prior, when Psalm 22 was written, there was no such thing as crucifixion, because the Romans hadn't even invented it yet. Stoning was the only known execution style to the Jews, and yet David wrote about the death to be suffered by the Lamb of God, not only before God came, but before that style of death was even invented, and at His last hour Christ repeats the words of David in Psalm 22:1 to remind those in attendance of the words of their patriarch David.

In a moment of astonishment the priests and Jewish leaders, the Pharisees, the Sanhedrin, and all those trained in the law, those who had made sure to crucify the Savior, hear these words as Christ, in His very last moments, draws their attention so that they know He is fulfilling this scripture as He suffered the death of crucifixion in order to save them. Jesus, the Lamb of God, who taketh away the sin of the world! You see, the Bible is all about prophecy, and Jesus is the fulfillment of that prophecy.

I was talking about this with my husband the other day, and he stopped me and said, "I love how God uses something that He knew was of utmost importance to them to reach them. He could have said something else, He could have called fire to storm out of heaven to prove to them that He was who He said He was, but instead Christ takes something that is personal to the very Jewish leaders who are persecuting Him; He takes a scripture that they all have memorized since they were children, a scripture pointing to the prophecy of the Messiah. He speaks to them in their own language and meets them where they are at." So with us, Christ always meets us where we are at.

The cross has to be the center of our quest for redemption. If Jesus existed, an issue that most scholars agree on (although there will always be conspiracy theorists who argue that it's dark even when the sun is shining brightly), then He cannot be a good teacher or a good man or a leader of a positive movement unless He was who He claimed to be.

Response to Critic Number Two

Claim: Jesus may have been a good man, but certainly was not God.

Reply: If Jesus wasn't God, then He was a pathological liar. Either He is God, as He said He was, or He wasn't a good man.

---

[1] www.beliefnet.com/Faiths/2005/03/Why-Jews-Don't-Accept-Jesus.aspx.

[2] Josephus *Antiquities* 20. 9.

[3] *Ibid.,* 18. 5.

[4] Tacitus *Annals* 15. 44.

[5] "The Apostle Paul," *Encyclopedia Britannica* (1997).

[6] www.tentmaker.org/Quotes/jesus-christ.htm.

[7] C. S. Lewis, *Mere Christianity* (New York: Harper Collins, 2001), p. 52.

Chapter 3

The Bible—One of the Best Works of Fiction

"To be fair, much of the Bible is not systematically evil but just plain weird, as you would expect of a chaotically cobbled-together anthology of disjointed documents, composed, revised, translated, distorted and 'improved' by hundreds of anonymous authors, editors and copyists, unknown to us and mostly unknown to each other, spanning nine centuries."[1]
—Richard Dawkins, author of *The God Delusion*

The biggest thing someone could do to add credibility to their position that God is a myth would be to disprove the Bible. We have all heard the age-old argument that the Bible was written by men, men make mistakes, and therefore, how could you ever assume the Bible to be inerrant? I had lunch with a friend of mine who was once a very active Seventh-day Adventist, but has lately turned agnostic. "There is plenty of research contradicting many biblical accounts," he said.

Our conversation is one of the reasons I decided to write this book. There were two other theistic believers at the table that day, and neither of them said anything. My friend explained his latest research, talked about his findings, and emphatically told us that the Bible was just too inaccurate to be true.

Now, it's not that the other two didn't want to respond; I am sure they did. I think the problem was just that they didn't know what to say. Unless a person is studying to become an evangelist or a religion teacher, Christians' understanding of the Bible is somewhat simplistic. We don't really question whether or not the passages are true; we just assume they are because our parents told us so, or our teachers did, and our friends at school all agreed. I've said it before, and I'll say it again: the biggest threat to our salvation is not an overabundance of scientific knowledge, but a lack of explanation for our own faith. If we don't know why we believe what we believe, it will be a cakewalk for someone else to silence us. You see, people don't decide not to believe in God just because there is no reason to believe; they don't believe because of things they have read or information they have gathered that has led them to think that belief in God is illogical.

In a class I am taking as a prerequisite to my doctoral program, I posted on the discussion board a few reasons I think it is important for Christians to research for themselves why they believe God is real. Another student responded to my comments by saying, "You cannot prove God. God is a matter of faith." I am convinced that this is the type of thinking that is causing our youth to leave the church in droves. God is not illogical, and we have to stop thinking that seeking knowledge is hurting our faith. Knowledge does not hurt faith—it improves it. Knowledge is good; it comes from God. It only makes sense to me that if God is the Creator of this universe, He would leave His fingerprints all over this place.

I recently watched a YouTube video in which a preacher named Louie Giglio explained how we can gain knowledge about God by paying attention to the human body. He said that he met a molecular biologist who, after learning the topic of his upcoming sermons, suggested that Giglio tell his listeners about laminin. Not being a molecular biologist, Giglio asked the scientist what laminin was and why he was so excited about it and insistent that he explain it to his listeners. The scientist went on to explain that laminins are important proteins in the basal lamina, which is a protein network serving as the foundation for almost all cells and organs. It is incredibly important to the human body because it basically holds all of our cells together. It is vital for the maintenance and survival of human body tissue. Faulty laminins can cause muscles and cells to form incorrectly. Without laminin we would literally fall apart.

After hearing all this, Giglio smiled and expressed his gratitude to the biologist for sharing, though he still didn't really understand why the scientist was so excited and so persistent that he tell his audience about laminin. "You have to promise me that when you get home, you will Google the image of laminin!" the scientist told Giglio.

"Sure," Giglio responded.

When Giglio got home, he remembered his encounter with the scientist, and when he had a moment he went to his computer and typed "laminin" into the search engine. His jaw dropped when he saw the image. "This is laminin?" he exclaimed. He couldn't wait to tell every audience about laminin. On the next page is a diagram of laminin.[2]

Louie Giglio was so excited when he saw laminin because the protein that is literally holding our body tissue together is in the shape of a cross. In the video Giglio goes on to say that he immediately thought of Colossians 1:16, 17, which says: "For in him all things were created: things in heaven

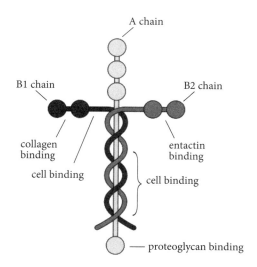

and on earth, visible and invisible, whether thrones or powers or rulers or authorities; all things have been created through him and for him. He is before all things, and in him all things hold together."

Is that not incredible? Could it be that just as laminin is holding you together at this very moment, Christ has also promised to hold you together through His most merciful act of sacrifice on the cross? I had a professor who once said that there are no coincidences, only Christ-incidences.

Paul writes in 1 Corinthians 8:6: "Yet for us there is but one God, the Father, from whom all things came and for whom we live; and there is but one Lord, Jesus Christ, through whom all things came and through whom we live."

Paul didn't know what a laminin molecule looked like when he penned these words, yet his portrayal of our relationship with Christ is undeniably powerful when paired with these molecular images. Could it be that the Author of our DNA left His mark in the very cells that are holding us together?

The Bible has a multitude of amazing discoveries much like this one that point to its supernatural inspiration and to uncanny revelations of future events through fulfilled prophecy. Daniel's explanation of Nebuchadnezzar's dream is probably the most popular depiction of fulfilled prophecy through biblical study.

In my research I found many more facts from modern archaeological digs than I ever dreamed existed. The first one I looked into was a discovery in a cave near Bethany. In the Gospel of Luke is an account of Jesus visiting the house of Mary and Martha (Luke 10:38-42). John's Gospel records the death, burial, and resurrection of Mary and Martha's brother, Lazarus, and specifies Bethany as the village in which they lived (John 11:1-44). In 1973 a number of ossuaries were found in a cave near Bethany, including some that had the names Mary, Martha, and Lazarus etched on them.[3] Some of the ossuaries had a cross etched on them as well, which might have indicated that these people were a part of the movement for Christ, or were Christians. (An ossuary is a coffin for bones that was used quite regularly between 20 B.C. and the Roman destruction of Jerusalem in A.D. 70. The dead body was placed in a cave, and once it had decayed, the bones were put in an ossuary.) Now, it can be noted that the names Mary, Martha, and Lazarus were common in biblical times, but what is the likelihood that individuals bearing these three common names were buried together in a cave near Bethany and had ossuaries with crosses on them? Crosses marking that they were followers of Christ.

The Bible records that Jesus was crucified, and biblical prophecies predicted His crucifixion before this type of execution even existed. Crucifixion was used by the Romans to put troublemakers to death. The individual was attached to a vertical wooden beam, to which a horizontal crossbeam was sometimes affixed, nails were put through his wrists and feet, and a sign was commonly hung at the top of the cross declaring the victim's crime to discourage others from committing the same crime.

In 1968 an ossuary was found in a tomb north of Jerusalem. Inscribed was the name Johanan. Inside were Johanan's bones, including a heel bone with a nail in it. Both leg bones had been broken. This corroborates the Bible's description of how the Romans crucified people.[4]

The Bible also says that Pontius Pilate was the Roman governor who ordered the death of Christ. Until the twentieth century, there was not much evidence supporting Pontius Pilate's existence, except that he was mentioned in the writings of Josephus and Tacitus. While some Italian archaeologists were excavating the theater in Caesarea in 1961, they found a stone inscribed with the name Pontius Pilate. The inscription seems to reference a temple that Pilate built honoring the Roman emperor Tiberius. Coins that date back to Pilate's rule have also been found.[5] Pontius Pilate existed, and this fact helps dispel the argument many make about the Bible being full of fables. On the contrary, the Bible is full of real people, historical figures, and actual events.

Many of the places and monuments established in the Bible are still standing today. For example, let's look at the narrative in Genesis 23:1-20 in which Abraham goes to find a place to bury his wife Sarah.

"Sarah lived to be a hundred and twenty-seven years old. She died at Kiriath Arba (that is, Hebron) in the land of Canaan, and Abraham went to mourn for Sarah and to weep over her.

"Then Abraham rose from beside his dead wife and spoke to the Hittites. He said, 'I am a foreigner and stranger among you. Sell me some property for a burial site here so I can bury my dead.'

"The Hittites replied to Abraham, 'Sir, listen to us. You are a mighty prince among us. Bury your dead in the choicest of our tombs. None of us will refuse you his tomb for burying your dead.'

"Then Abraham rose and bowed down before the people of the land, the Hittites. He said to them, 'If you are willing to let me bury my dead, then listen to me and intercede with Ephron son of Zohar on my behalf so he will sell me the cave of Machpelah, which belongs to him and is at the end of his field. Ask him to sell it to me for the full price as a burial site among you.'

"Ephron the Hittite was sitting among his people and he replied to Abraham in the hearing of all the Hittites who had come to the gate. . . . 'No, my lord,' he said. 'Listen to me; I give you the field, and I give you the cave that is in it. I give it to you in the presence of my people. Bury your dead.'

"Again Abraham bowed down before the people of the land and he said to Ephron in their hearing, 'Listen to me, if you will. I will pay the price of the field. Accept it from me so I can bury my dead there.'

"Ephron answered Abraham, 'Listen to me, my lord; the land is worth four hundred shekels of silver, but what is that between you and me? Bury your dead.'

"Abraham agreed to Ephron's terms and weighed out for him the price he had named in the hearing of the Hittites: four hundred shekels of silver, according to the weight current among the merchants.

"So Ephron's field in Machpelah near Mamre—both the field and the cave in it, and all the trees within the borders of the field—was deeded to Abraham as his property in the presence of all the Hittites who had come to the gate of the city. Afterward Abraham buried his wife Sarah in the cave in the field of Machpelah near Mamre (which is at Hebron) in the land of Canaan. So the field and the cave in it were deeded to Abraham by the Hittites as a burial site."

The site in this biblical reference still stands today, and its very presence should silence the lips of skeptics. About 2,000 years ago a monument covering the burial place of Abraham was built by Herod the Great.

"When modern tourists visit Hebron, they focus almost exclusively on the Tomb of the Patriarchs, a magnificent shrine built 2,000 years ago during the Herodian period over the traditional site of the Cave of Machpelah. The Bible tells us the patriarchs Abraham, Isaac and Jacob and the matriarchs Sarah, Rebecca and Leah were all buried there. The relative dimensions of the structure, and even the style of its ashlar masonry, are similar to the great Temple Mount enclosure wall that Herod built in Jerusalem, on the site where Solomon had built the First Temple and where the exiles returning from Babylon built a more modest structure that Herod replaced. More visitors depart unaware that just a thousand yards to the west, easily visible from the shrine, is the mound that was the site of the ancient Biblical city of Hebron. The hill, called Jebel er-Rumeide in Arabic, rises prominently above the surrounding buildings in the center of the modern city."[6]

At this point I would like to turn to other outside literature that supports the biblical account of Jesus' crucifixion, specifically the Babylonian Talmud. The Talmud is a set of writings by various Jewish rabbis that provide commentary on a multitude of subjects. It is believed that the Talmud was completed about the sixth century. In it we find references to Jesus. "On the eve of Passover they hanged Jesus the Nazarene. And a herald went out before him for forty days, saying: 'He is going to be stoned, because he practiced sorcery and enticed and led Israel astray. Anyone who knows anything in his favor, let him come and plead in his behalf.' But, not having found anything in his favor, they hanged him on the eve of Passover."[7]

Here I would remind you of the quote from *The God Delusion,* by Richard Dawkins, that opens this chapter: "To be fair, much of the Bible is not systematically evil but just plain weird, as you would expect of a chaotically cobbled-together anthology of disjointed documents, composed, revised, translated, distorted and 'improved' by hundreds of anonymous authors, editors and copyists, unknown to us and mostly unknown to each other, spanning nine centuries."[8]

Dawkins is intelligent and extremely accomplished, but when it comes to his writings about the Bible, I fear he was a bit out of his element. There is no book or ancient manuscript that even remotely compares to the

Bible in both prophetic accuracy and archaeological confirmation. When compared to other writings, the Bible is in a league of its own. We have 663 original manuscripts of Homer's *Iliad*, the second most preserved literary work, compared to more than 5,000 copies of the New Testament. The Dead Sea scrolls also provide us with some remarkable evidence for the reliability of the Bible.[9] It is interesting to note that scholars regard the ancient text of Julius Caesar's *Commentaries on the Gallic War* as authentic even though just 10 copies have been preserved, the earliest one dating to about 1,000 years after its original composition. And yet the authenticity of the Bible is questioned.

There are 764 disputed lines in *The Iliad,* and just 40 disputed lines in all of the New Testament. Homer's classic contains approximately 15,600 lines, with 764 of those lines called into question. Mathematically, this represents about 5 percent of the entire text. Compare this with the New Testament, of which only 40 lines of approximately 20,000 are disputed. Mathematically, these 40 lines represent one quarter of 1 percent of the entire text.[10] We should note that these 40 disputed lines are mainly translation errors that have arisen because the Bible has been translated from Greek, Hebrew, and Aramaic. Where are the critics for Homer? They are silent.

The renowned biblical scholar F. F. Bruce said this of the book that critics would like to convince you is errant: "There is no body of ancient literature in the world which enjoys such a wealth of good textual attestation as the New Testament."[11] What I have come to realize is that the Bible, Jesus, and Christianity will be disregarded as long as there is a devil working to ensnare people. As long as there is sin, there will be disagreement on the power and glory of the Holy Book, no matter how much evidence exists to the contrary. There is more evidence in the case for Christ than any other truth in this world, and yet there are more skeptics than believers. Sometimes you may feel as though you are the only one working hard to advance His kingdom. Sometimes you feel as if it is you against the world. I have learned two things that I cling to in these moments of frustration. The first: keep trying anyway. The second: you are not alone.

You see, there is a certain burden that comes with what you are learning in these pages: you must share it. It seems fitting to end this chapter by offering encouragement through a biblical story, the story of Elijah as narrated in 1 Kings. Elijah has just experienced his greatest moment: fire falling from heaven to accept his offering of atonement on behalf of the people of Israel. He has just stood witness for the one true God as hundreds of Baal's prophets chanted, danced, screamed to Baal—and even mutilated themselves—in hopes that he would accept their sacrifice. However, Baal was silent while God allowed His presence to resound over Mount Carmel.

Right after Elijah experiences this spiritual high, he flees when he discovers that Jezebel has demanded his life. First Kings 19:9 picks up the story as Elijah finds refuge in a cave. "There he went into a cave and spent the night. And the word of the Lord came to him: 'What are you doing here, Elijah?' "

I love this! There is a myriad of things God could have said here. He could have chastised Elijah for running. He could have pointed out that He had just affirmed Elijah in front of thousands of people in an event that could easily be described as the greatest moment of Elijah's life. He could have punished him for showing such a lack of faith by running at all. Instead, He simply asks Elijah, "What are you doing here?"

Perhaps God has asked you this same question. Instead of abandonment, instead of punishment, instead of reproach because of your missed step or because you hid from His call, He simply turns to you and says with the love only a parent can bestow, "What are you doing here? Don't you know that I have somewhere else for you to be? Don't you know I created you with a purpose? Don't you know that I have a destiny for you? I have to ask, What exactly are you doing here?"

In verse 10 we see how alone Elijah feels—and that God knows it. Elijah says, "I have been very zealous for the Lord God Almighty. The Israelites have rejected your covenant, torn down your altars, and put your prophets to death with the sword. I am the only one left, and now they are trying to kill me too."

Then we see God respond to him in verse 15 by saying, "Go back the way you came, and go to the Desert of Damascus." After He gives Elijah a few instructions, He leaves him with this last response to Elijah's declaration that he is alone: "Yet I reserve seven thousand in Israel—all whose knees have not bowed down to Baal and whose mouths have not kissed him" (verse 18).

Elijah was not alone. Seven thousand other people were faithful to God and were living examples to their idolatrous neighbors. Likewise, you are not alone. I challenge you—I know we are only three chapters in here, but we have a lot of ground to cover—to stop where you are and make it a point to share what you've learned. Satan is busy collecting corpses, so even if no one seems as if they are interested, keep trying. And if you are already burned out, if you've already tried to connect with and tell others about this friend you've found in Jesus and you've been rejected, let me remind you of the words God whispered to Samuel in 1 Samuel 8:7: "It is not you they have rejected, but they have rejected me." You are not alone. You have a mission to accomplish, a bundle of good news to deliver to anyone who will hear you. God is lovingly nudging you right here where you sit in frustration, and He is asking you, "What are you doing here?"

Response to Critic Number Three

Claim: There is plenty of research that proves that the Bible is inaccurate.

Reply: We have 663 original manuscripts of Homer's *Iliad*, the second most preserved literary work, in comparison to more than 5,000 copies of the New Testament, but no one disputes the *Iliad*. Discontentment with the Bible should not center on whether or not it is reliable. It is reliable, and since it is, the question should be What is the invitation it is providing in my life?

---

[1] Richard Dawkins, *The God Delusion* (New York: Bantam Press, 2006).

[2] Laminin photo: lightandlifegraphics.com, retrieved Mar. 1, 2012.

[3] Craig L. Blomberg, *The Historical Reliability of John's Gospel* (Downer's Grove, Ill.: InterVarsity Press, 2001), p. 165.

[4] *Ibid.,* pp. 265, 266.

[5] Alan Millard, *Discoveries From the Bible* (Oxford: Lion Publishing, 1997), pp. 226ff.

[6] Jeffrey R. Chadwick, "Discovering Hebron: the City of the Patriarchs Slowly Yields Its Secrets," *Biblical Archaeology Review*, September/October 2005.

[7] Joel B. Green, Scot McKnight, I. Howard Marshall, eds., "Jesus in Non-Christian Sources," *Dictionary of Jesus and the Gospels* (Downer's Grove, Ill.: InterVarsity Press, 1992), p. 367.

[8] Dawkins.

[9] Josh McDowell, *The New Evidence That Demands a Verdict* (Thomas Nelson Pub., 1999), pp. 71-73.

[10] *Ibid.*

[11] F. F. Bruce, *The Books and the Parchments: How We Got Our English Bible* (Old Tappan, N.J.: Fleming H. Revell Co., 1963).

Chapter 4

If God Is Real,
Then He Is Misogynistic

"It'll be a cold day in hell
before I get my theology from a woman."
—Jack Schaap

It is one of the biggest criticisms of Christ, and the Bible, that God is sexist; therefore, why in the world would any woman become a Christian? I once heard a lecturer who was explaining the many problems with the Christian creed argue that any woman who would ascribe herself to a belief system that ultimately degrades women is a fool. I had to ask myself while jotting down notes on his rhetoric if there was any truth to what he was saying. Does the Bible place women in an inferior position to men?

I cannot lie. I have heard some Christian men make the claim that women, because of sin, are simply lower on the totem pole than their male counterparts. I have also heard Christian women say that they would never vote for a woman for political office or for any position of authority if there was a suitable man to fill that same role. In other words, they believe that if there is a man available, we should always pick the man to fill a position of leadership because men are better leaders. They then use the Bible to back up their statements.

Jack Schaap, who was once the pastor of the First Baptist Church in Hammond, Indiana, said, "A woman didn't write this book. Not one woman wrote the Scriptures right here. A man wrote the Bible—got it from God. A man hung on the cross. His name is Jesus Christ, and God called a man to lead the church here. Hey! I'm glad I'm a man!"

While Schaap is glad to be a man, I am quite glad that Schaap is not my pastor and that I am not a member of his church. I am worried, however, about the people he is misleading with such statements, people who are not familiar with the Bible but are familiar with people who profess to be Christians. The Bible warns of false teachers who lead many astray through ignorance. Second Timothy 3:13 says that "evildoers and impostors will go from bad to worse, deceiving and being deceived."

As I listened intently to this lecturer who called any woman foolish who chooses to promote a faith that demotes her value to society, I found myself agreeing with him. The Bible I read, however, does not degrade the value of women. When you study religion academically, they teach you about the principle of *sola scriptura,* comparing scripture with scripture in order to allow the Bible to explain itself. We cannot take one text and draw a conclusion from it if that conclusion does not fit with everything else we see in Scripture. Another issue to be aware of while studying Scripture is translations, because words in Greek and Hebrew may have multiple meanings.

Much of the Bible was written in masculine language. In Romans 3:28 Paul writes that "a man is justified by faith" (KJV). Should we then infer that women are not justified by faith? What about Matthew 5:9? "Blessed are the peacemakers, for they shall be called sons of God" (NKJV). Are women peacemakers not the children of God? In John 14:21 it says: "He who has My commandments and keeps them, it is he who loves Me. And he who loves Me will be loved by My Father, and I will love him and manifest Myself to him" (NKJV). Was Jesus speaking to men only when He spoke of obedience to His commandments?

It seems there are relatively little-known issues concerning gender-inclusive language within our canonical Scriptures that have sparked much debate. Though some texts can be relatively straightforward when compared to the original Hebrew or Greek contexts, others are not, and this can be difficult when trying to understand various teachings. The nature of language can become very complex when sifting through translations. Difficulties arise primarily when trying to identify which situations were meant to be inclusive of both genders and which were not. With situations in which things are not as straightforward, one must study carefully to delineate the historical and literary context. This can be a long and painstaking process requiring much research and prayer.

Context becomes extremely important to interpretation, and interpretation is not always as exclusive or inclusive as one might like. One argument made is that the Old Testament did not have women priests; therefore women are limited in what they can and cannot do when it comes to a spiritual calling. This places women in an inferior role spiritually. What we are forgetting, however, when using this argument is that in a way we are comparing apples to oranges. In ancient Israel the right to the priesthood was not available to those who felt "called" to ministry.

The right was restricted to a group within the tribe of Levi, namely, the descendants of Aaron as prescribed in Exodus 28:41.

The reservation of the Levite tribe to do the work of the tabernacle/Temple is attributed to their return and commitment to the true God after all the tribes had sought the comfort of an image to worship and created the golden calf (Exodus 32; Numbers 3:6-13). The Bible is not clear on the reason Aaron was selected for the privilege of such leadership, other than the fact that he was Moses' brother and worked alongside him during the exodus from Egypt and afterward. God did appoint Aaron to be Moses' spokesperson to Israel and to Pharaoh; however, Aaron remained subordinate to Moses.

I have read books in which the authors reference this relationship between prophet and priest to assert that even the priest is dependent upon prophecy. In other words, the hierarchical order would be prophet first and priest second. If true, this is clearly an important claim because of the beliefs of the Seventh-day Adventist Church in regard to Ellen White. This is a church that has been led and guided by a woman prophet.

Christ gave us pastors, or priests, to help shepherd the flock until He returns. These leaders pray and hope they are discerning Christ's messages aptly and relaying them to the people correctly. Prophets, however, have heard His audible voice with their own ears or have seen visions of Christ's messages with their own eyes. God has decided to open their eyes and ears to receive messages that are of supreme importance. If Christ did not believe women to be an extremely precious and valuable part of His creation, He would have to exclude them from prophecy.

I read a book titled *Women in Ministry* for one of my classes. Chapter 2, which deals with the absence of women in the priesthood in ancient Israel, was written by Jacques B. Doukhan. He explains the lack of women in priesthood by explaining what was going on in the nations surrounding Israel. Female priests were common, as was prostitution and the worship of goddesses. Doukhan believes that the lack of female priests could be a response to the neighboring pagan practices; in effect the priesthood "became stricter as a reflex of defense against Baalist contaminations" in an effort to keep God's people out of sexual immorality.[1]

The priesthood of ancient Israel had three primary duties: administration, prophecy, and dealing with the sacrifices and services in the tabernacle/Temple. After looking at these three functions, Doukhan concludes that we have biblical evidence of women in Israel performing two of the three duties. Women did serve as judges and administrators, we see examples of them in a prophetic role, and we find references in Joel and Acts of them having visions and/or dreams. From this we understand that the only function barred to women and excluding them from the priesthood was the practice of sacrificial rites, although women prepared sacrificial meals and were present at the ceremonies.

The Bible does not explain why women were not allowed to perform sacrifices, but we can use other biblical references to infer various reasons, a woman's monthly ritual uncleanness being one. Another possible explanation is that women are responsible for providing life, thus life and death (by sacrifice) have no relationship to each other. Doukhan concludes the chapter with a query: if the only basis for preventing women from being priests in ancient Israel was their inability to perform sacrifices, how does this exclude women from pastoral (priestly) ministry nowadays, considering that the Lamb has been slain and no further ceremonial sacrificial practices take place?[2]

Another argument about the differing biblical roles of men and women is found in Genesis within the Creation story. To have a clear understanding of both sides of the debate, we must first turn to the scriptures at the center of the discussion. In Genesis 1 and 2 we see the Creation plan before the Fall of humanity into sin. Genesis 1:27 gives us an understanding of how God created humankind: "So God created mankind in his own image, in the image of God he created them; male and female he created them."

Here we see that man and woman are equal before sin entered the world. God makes no distinction between the sexes and says that both are created in His image. However, the viewpoint of the Council on Biblical Manhood and Womanhood concerning pre-sin gender roles is that man was created first and woman second, which suggests that the first is superior to the second. Also, woman was created for the purpose of being the man's assistant. Man was lonely, so God created woman to soothe his loneliness. The woman's creation from the man's rib suggests that she is dependent on man for life and also implies that the woman holds a subordinate position to the man. The man also names the woman, which asserts his authority over her.

Christians for Biblical Equality take a different perspective when evaluating these same two chapters. Richard Davidson writes in his contribution to *Women in Ministry*: "The movement in Genesis 2, if anything, is not from superior to inferior, but from incompleteness to completeness. Woman is created as the climax, the culmination of the story. She is the crowning work of creation."[3]

To address the idea that woman was formed for the sake of man, we turn back to Genesis 2:18, which reads: "The Lord God said, 'It is not good for the man to be alone. I will make a helper suitable for him.'" The word "helper" in English suggests a superior and inferior connotation. However, Davidson argues that in Hebrew there is no such connotation. In fact, he claims that the Hebrew word for "helper" is a relational one that suggests a beneficial relationship of one to the other, without the existence of superiority or inferiority. This suggests that Eve is Adam's counterpart, an equal to him, and that both benefit each other. Together they experience completeness.

In answer to those who perceive the symbolism of woman being formed from man's rib as a suggestion that she is indeed inferior to man and dependent upon him for life, Davidson says the fact that Eve was derived from Adam does not suggest superiority of Adam to Eve any more than the fact that Adam was derived from the ground suggests that Adam is inferior to the ground. Davidson also points out that man was asleep during the creation of woman. This he believes was intentional on God's part in order to suggest that man had no part in Eve's creation—God was the architect of Eve just as He was of Adam.

I love how complex Scripture really is. Everything has meaning; nothing is written to provide fluff for what would be a white page otherwise. We can also see through other biblical commentary that God always provides us with behind-the-scenes knowledge for a reason. My husband likes to remind me when I'm reading Scripture that I should dig deeper every time I read the name of a king who died, because the author is giving me the name of that king for a reason. The king's name tells the reader something about what was going on in Israel at the time a particular prophet was called.

We should read the Bible and ask why certain information is provided, rather than reading just to read. My spiritual life has been completely renovated since I began reading Scripture to understand better who God is. When I see how complex Scripture is, I am reminded that only a fool would suggest that it is not inspired—there is simply too much gold there for it not to be treasure. Someone who says the Bible is not holy has clearly never studied it. You could spend your entire life studying the Bible and still not scratch the surface of how intricate and meaningful every word is.

When the Bible tells us that Adam was asleep for the creation of Eve, it tells us this for a reason.

The symbolism of woman's creation around man's rib actually suggests equality rather than inferiority. Ellen White writes in *Patriarchs and Prophets*: "Eve was created from a rib taken from the side of Adam, signifying that she was not to control him as the head, nor to be trampled under his feet as an inferior, but to stand by his side as an equal, to be loved and protected by him."[4]

In Genesis 2:23 we witness the Bible's first form of poetry when Adam first sees Eve: "The man said, 'This is now bone of my bones and flesh of my flesh; she shall be called "woman," for she was taken out of man.'" None of these words denote submission or inferiority. This is the imagery of love and affection.

Some have argued that the above text suggests that Adam is superior because he calls her "woman." Davidson argues that Adam does not name her at this point; he simply defines her using a genetic identification of that which is different from himself. Woman is not a personal name given to Eve. Also, Adam simply restates what God has already done, since Adam had no part in the formation of Eve. Adam is saying that since she was taken out of man by God, she should be called, "out of man." This suggests that man did not determine what the woman was, but out of joy and excitement proclaimed what God has done in completing the picture of humanity. Davidson points out that it is after the Fall that Adam names her "Eve." This does suggest headship and authority, but this was not present at Creation.

We look to the third chapter of Genesis to see what happened after the Fall. The judgment pronounced upon the woman is related in verse 16: "To the woman he [God] said, 'I will make your pains in childbearing very severe; with painful labor you will give birth to children. Your desire will be for your husband, and he will rule over you.'" Davidson asserts that the last two lines are of significance for a proper understanding of the nature of the sexual relationship between husband and wife presumed throughout the rest of Scripture. He goes on to list five major views concerning these verses.

The first view is that the original plan for equality is distorted as a result of sin and that it is only after we see sin that we find that man is to rule over woman.

The second view is that through the woman's curse, the man will be a helper for her. This view interprets the verses as saying that although a woman will have difficulty in childbirth, she will remain eager for her husband and he will rule over her. The sense here is that he will be a care provider and helper to her, but not that he is to oppress her.

The third view is that man was to rule over woman after sin entered the picture, but that was to be abolished once Christ gave the gospel. They view this submission not as a permanent one, but one that is in place until Christ's sacrifice on the cross.

The fourth view coincides much with the third view, except it holds that God has now presented His new normative pattern for husband and wife after the Fall.

The fifth view agrees with that of the second view, which says that the husband's rule over the wife is a blessing and not a curse. This view translates the word "rule" differently, as "to resemble" or "to be like," which again emphasizes the equality of husband and wife. It also can be taken in this view that man's rule over woman is of a sexual nature: wives often must concede to husbands' sexual advances.

Davidson argues that in this perception, the judgment against Eve is a curse that has been fulfilled and that can be seen just by looking at history. Women are still unequal to men in the workplace, and women are still burdened with hardships that men simply do not face. He also says that none of the other judgments were removed at the cross, so the judgment against woman should stay intact. His view, however, is that this was not part of God's original plan but is the result of sin.

He writes: "This is not to say that it is inappropriate for humankind to seek to roll back the judgments/curses and get back as much as possible to God's original plan by advancing in obstetrics to relieve unnecessary hard labor and delivery; by agricultural and technological advances to relieve unnecessary hard labor in farming, by scientific and medical advances to delay the process of death."[5] The author argues that the principle of turning back as much as we can to God's original plan is not seen as wrong anywhere else, but only when dealing with equality between a man and a woman in marriage. His point is that we need to keep harmony in the home, but to do so through equality. If we do not have a problem with advancements in culture and technology that change the curse God placed on man and woman after sin, why should we not move with the culture and advance women as well?

The author agrees that after the Fall, man was meant to be the head of the woman in the home as punishment for her role in causing man to sin.

Ellen White writes: "In the creation God had made her [Eve] the equal of Adam. Had they remained obedient to God—in harmony with His great law of love—they would ever have been in harmony with each other; but sin had brought discord, and now their union could be maintained and harmony preserved only by submission on the part of the one or the other. Eve had been the first in transgression; and she had fallen into temptation by separating from her companion, contrary to the divine direction. It was by her solicitation that Adam sinned, and she was now placed in subjection to her husband. Had the principles enjoined in the law of God been cherished by the fallen race, this sentence, though growing out of the results of sin, would have proved a blessing to them; but man's abuse of the supremacy thus given him has too often rendered the lot of woman very bitter and made her life a burden."[6]

Davidson goes on to say that the word translated "rule" in Genesis 3:16 is not the same as the word used in the context of Adam ruling over the animals. The word translated "rule" to describe the relationship between Adam and Eve does indicate submission and subjection but in the sense of servant leadership, meaning "to give comfort, protect, care for, and love."[7]

The curse of pain in childbirth is then followed by a blessing. Essentially, even though the woman will be in pain during labor, which would make her not want to continue having sexual relations with her husband, she will continue to yearn for him. This sexual bond will help keep the union from sin, and the man will protect and care for her.

Davidson concludes by saying that the submission of wife to husband is apparent in the marriage relationship, and that nowhere in the verses does it suggest that there is a submission of woman to man outside of this context, a point that is crucial when considering the attitude of the church toward women and whether or not God is sexist. Davidson says that "any attempt to extend this prescription beyond the husband-wife relationship is not warranted by the text."[8]

I think this point is of vast importance, because if marriage is done correctly, there should be absolutely no problem with male headship in the marriage relationship. If man and woman become "bone of bones, and flesh of flesh," then they are unified. They experience and share a tenderness and respect for each other that no other relationship in the human experience can re-create. Why then would it be bothersome to anyone that men who love their wives unconditionally experience a type of leadership over them in the marriage relationship? I believe the only reason this would ruffle anyone's feathers is that there are so many bad examples of marriage. There are so many unloving husbands that the thought of the Bible stating man's leadership in the marriage union is scary. We have to remember, though, what marriage was intended to do. It was intended to bring partnership and joy to each other. It was intended to complete the image of Creation. Marriage was never meant to be oppressive.

Though headship and leadership clearly exists between a man and woman within a marriage, it does not exclude women from positions of authority. We can look to Deborah, the prophet and judge in Judges 4-5. Deborah exercises headship over men as a political and military leader in Israel and is on equal footing with Barak, the male general.

But what about the position of women as described in the New Testament? First Timothy 2:11, 12 reads: "A woman should learn in quietness and full submission. I do not permit a woman to teach or to assume authority over a man; she must be quiet." Davidson argues that the Greek words should be translated as "husband" and "wife" instead of the generic "man" and "woman," as evidence strongly supports that conclusion. Davidson closes his chapter by saying that a headship/submission policy does exist, but only within the confines of marriage, and that there is no prohibition of women holding positions of leadership outside of marriage. In other words, men and women are equal in the workplace, in the church, and in school. Only in marriage—and we should remember that marriage was meant to be a completely selfless and loving relationship—do we see headship and authority of men over women.

I've also heard it said that because Adam was created first, God was showing preference to men over women because men were His "firstborn." I agree that firstborn sons were biblically significant, but this can hardly be seen as a rule for handling biblical teachings. Off the top of my head I can think of several nonfirstborns whom God favored. Isaac was technically Abraham's second son, as Ishmael's birth preceded his. Jacob was not the firstborn, yet was chosen by God as the father of the Israelite nation. Joseph, who was crucial to the preservation of the future nation of Israel, was Jacob's eleventh son. When Jacob blessed Joseph's sons, Manasseh and Ephraim, he blessed Ephraim, the younger son, with a greater blessing than Manasseh, the elder. Hundreds of years later Aaron's little brother Moses was clearly God's spokesperson to and leader of Israel. This leads me to conclude that God makes His choices on an individual basis and not by the order of their birth.

Others say that because Eve sinned first, women are inferior. It is true that Eve sinned first, but she was tricked into sin, whereas Adam chose to sin. Afraid that Eve would be lost to him, Adam chose her over God. Eve was tempted by the most intelligent being God had created; Satan was, and is, the greatest manipulator and liar in the universe. She was fooled, but Adam was not; his was a conscious decision to sin. Satan still works to tempt us these two ways. We make choices to sin and we are tricked into sin, all of which separate us from Christ. Again, the Bible is providing us with examples of how sin works, and Satan always uses one of these two agencies: trickery or choice.

Susan T. Foh discusses the relationship between man and woman in Eden as being something hard to explain now because of our corrupted view of domination:

"We know only the arbitrariness, the domination, the arrogance that even the best boss/underling relationship has. But in Eden, it was different. It really was. The man and the woman knew each other as equals, both in the image of God, and thus each with a personal relationship to God. Neither doubted the worth of the other nor of himself/herself. Each was to perform his/her task in a different way, the man as the head, and the woman as the helper. They operated as truly one flesh, one person. In one body, does the rib rebel against or envy the head?"[9]

I agree with the idea that the man should be the head of the house. In the ideal relationship, one in which the husband loves his wife deeply, it does not seem to matter who the head is, because where there is love, there is peace. In a marriage like this, the husband cares about what his wife thinks and takes into account her feelings and opinions. His headship of the family is a blessing to his wife and children because they can trust him to protect and take care of them.

Is God misogynistic or sexist? I don't believe the Bible provides us with anything to support that idea. At the end of the day, even with mountains of research and scholarly knowledge to use when approaching questionable topics in Scripture, we have to look at what we know and understand of God's character. God is love.

Ellen White writes of the inestimable worth of even one human being in God's eyes: "One soul is precious, very precious, in the sight of God. Christ would have died for one soul in order that that one might live through the eternal ages."[10] Are we to assume that if this one person was a woman, the redemption story would have turned out any differently? Of course not! God loves His children regardless of their gender.

The biggest reason I know that God is not sexist is that I know how much He loves me, and I am a woman. I know this because I have seen Him fight for me tooth and nail and pursue me relentlessly. He spent time and energy on me because of the intense love and adoration He has for all His children. God is not sexist or misogynistic, and I find it insulting that anyone would call Him such names. The only names humans should be calling God behind His back are names that refer to His holiness and love.

Response to Critic Number Four

Claim: If God is real, He is misogynistic.

Reply: Can you tell me on which biblical reference you are basing your statement? If you don't mind, I'd like to discuss the background on that verse—there's more than meets the eye.

---

[1] Nancy Vyhmeister, ed., *Women in Ministry* (Berrien Springs, Mich.: Andrews University Press, 1998).

[2] *Ibid.*

[3] *Ibid.*

[4] Ellen G. White, *Patriarchs and Prophets* (Mountain View, Calif.: Pacific Press Pub. Assn., 1890), p. 46.

[5] Vyhmeister.

[6] E. G. White, pp. 58, 59.

[7] Vyhmeister.

[8] *Ibid.*

[9] Susan T. Foh, *Women and the Word of God* (Phillipsburg, N.J.: Presbyterian & Reformed Pub. Co., 1978), p. 62.

[10] Ellen G. White, *Testimonies for the Church* (Mountain View, Calif.: Pacific Press Pub. Assn., 1948), vol. 8, p. 73.

Chapter 5

Virgin Is Another Word for *Loser*

"There is more to sex appeal than just measurements. I don't need a bedroom to prove my womanliness. I can convey just as much sex appeal, picking apples off a tree or standing in the rain."
—Audrey Hepburn, actress[1]

Why would *virgin* be another word for *loser?* Well, for starters we have movies such as *The 40-Year-Old Virgin,* which is about a guy who can't seem to lose his virginity. Any guy or girl who is still a virgin in this day and age is viewed as having some type of social malfunction. I had a friend who used to say, "I'm skeptical of people who didn't like high school, girls with no other girlfriends, and virgins." Virginity in today's world is no longer a symbol of purity and beauty, but of awkwardness. Anyone who is anyone is having sex; therefore, someone who isn't must have some weird disorder. Sex is everywhere, even in our church schools.

I recently read an article by Bonnie Rochman in *Time* magazine about the effects of sex on teenagers. The study was done by researchers at Penn State University who began tracking a group of 434 first-year college students. Over a four-year period they provided these students with questionnaires four separate times. The questions addressed the student's satisfaction with his or her appearance. During the four-year study 100 of the students had sex for the first time. The researchers then concentrated on those 100 students because they wanted to find the correlation between premarital sex and self-esteem. They found that the women's first sexual encounters had a negative effect on their self-esteem. Men, however, tended to have higher views of their own appearance afterward.[2]

A study by the Barna Research Group, a nonprofit organization that researches primarily the Christian population, found that more than two thirds of Americans in their 20s and 30s believe that cohabitation is morally OK and that most of those in that age group believe it is not wrong to have extramarital sex.[3] What blew my mind was realizing there was hardly any difference in the way *Christian* young people responded. Fifty-nine percent of young adult Christians said that cohabitation was morally acceptable.

I don't usually like to talk about sex, because I feel as though it is a subject everyone has already heard about and is basically desensitized to. I always thought the issue of premarital sex was a no-brainer—everyone knew it was a sin, and it would be pointless to waste time harping on it because people know and do it anyway. But I was shocked to find out that most Christians don't know. The world has succeeded in ridding Christians of their consciences and biblical knowledge, and that is scary. Because a large percentage of you who read this book will genuinely not see what the issue with premarital sex is, I have to address it. Don't worry, I am not going to use the typical approach here. Let me walk you through the Heather Thompson Day understanding of what the problem is with premarital (and extramarital) sex.

The first article we looked at in this chapter showed that premarital sex hurts women's self-esteem. I believe that it also affects men's self-esteem, especially those who profess to believe in Jesus Christ. All sin hurts us; it separates us from God—especially those sins that appeal to our carnal appetite. Satan will use sex—or anything else, for that matter—to separate you from God, because he wants to make you believe you are unworthy of God's love. I am sure nothing agitates the devil more than the fact that God, a God whom he has known personally, a God whose holiness he has witnessed firsthand, that same God is in love with a group of degenerated misfits called humans. Jealousy was what first caused Lucifer to sin. He is still jealous. He is jealous of God, and he is jealous of us. He is desperate, then, to entice us into rejecting the best gift we have ever received. After all, in his eyes we don't deserve it.

Here's the thing. Whether you've had extramarital sex with one person or 100, when you recognize that your sexual appetite has hurt your spiritual growth and you want to turn away from sin, God will purify you. I don't care what your Bible teacher, your neighbor, or the girls or guys at school have said about you. You are a child of Jesus Christ, and He's all about restoration. I tell you this because I don't want you to read on with your head bowed in shame. Life is all about choices, and the only thing more important than the ones you have already made are the ones you will make. There's no shame at the foot of the cross, only love.

So what reasons do Christian young adults give for sexual freedom?

The Bible is simply too old. Those stances on sexual purity are not relevant anymore. Actually, in Bible times, everyone got married at 13, so they didn't struggle with sexual purity. If only we could update those archaic pages; I think God would understand.

First Corinthians 6:9, 10 says: "Or do you not know that wrongdoers will not inherit the kingdom of God? Do not be deceived: neither the sexually immoral nor idolaters nor adulterers nor men who have sex with men nor thieves nor the greedy nor drunkards nor slanderers nor swindlers will inherit the kingdom of God."

Second Corinthians 12:21 says: "I am afraid that when I come again my God will humble me before you, and I will be grieved over many who have sinned earlier and have not repented of the impurity, sexual sin and debauchery in which they have indulged."

Colossians 3:5, 6 says: "Put to death, therefore, whatever belongs to your earthly nature: sexual immorality, impurity, lust, evil desires and greed, which is idolatry. Because of these, the wrath of God is coming."

Hebrews 13:4 reads: "Marriage should be honored by all, and the marriage bed kept pure, for God will judge the adulterer and all the sexually immoral."

So when it comes to sex, the Bible is clear that we should strive to remain pure; and by pure we mean one man and one woman within a marriage relationship. But is Scripture outdated?

Here's the thing about the Bible: either you believe it, or you don't. Either God is who He says He is, or He isn't. Even though our generation has a hard time accepting a Bible that makes right and wrong crystal clear, God does not change. He is the same yesterday, today, and tomorrow. His word always stands. If we want to get rid of sexual morality because we find it unrealistic, we have to do away with all of His commandments. Whether a person struggles with adultery, theft, deceit, violence, a covetous nature, or one of the other roots of all sin listed in the Decalogue, it's a test of character to keep God's commandments. Being a Christian isn't easy. Following God rarely is.

So why would God want sex to remain within the boundary of marriage? Well, let's look around at our fallen world and see how well we are doing when we treat sex casually. AIDS and sexually transmitted diseases (STDs) are everywhere. The Centers for Disease Control and Prevention (CDC) estimates that young people between the ages of 15 and 24 account for nearly half of all newly acquired STDs—and that age group makes up only 25 percent of the "sexually experienced population."[4] The AIDS epidemic has crippled entire nations. And what happens when single moms raise babies by themselves as a result of casual sex? Those kids miss out on one of the most influential components of society: daddies. Research shows that the absence of the biological father in the home is a leading factor of both violence and incarceration.[5]

I recently read a story about a woman who worked in prison ministry. She thought it would be nice to have Mother's Day cards available to the inmates. She asked a card company to donate Mother's Day cards to the cause, and after spreading the word, she opened up shop. However, she quickly ran out of cards. There were more inmates wanting to send tokens of love and affection to their mothers on Mother's Day than she had cards to hold their thoughts of appreciation. She was thrilled to help, so one month later when Father's Day rolled around, she asked the card company to donate more cards. The company donated cards again, and after spreading the word, the volunteer set up shop, ready to provide Father's Day cards to any inmate who wanted one.

The author of the story put it this way: "Do you know how many of those felons, many with a history of violence, asked for a card this time? Not one. Not a single prisoner wanted to express love to his dad. And that's when the woman learned that such men usually carry a deep resentment, even hatred, toward their fathers, many of whom were absent from their sons.

"Children with active fathers are less likely to commit juvenile crimes than children with inactive fathers. The chances that a child will commit crimes as an adult also diminish when he grows up with an actively involved father." [6]

Some casualties of casual sex never take their first breath. The CDC's Abortion Surveillance report for 2009, the latest year for which statistics for legal abortion were available at presstime, shows that one in five pregnancies was terminated.[7] Take a minute to absorb that information: 20 percent of Americans conceived in 2009 wound up in the bottom of an abortion clinic's garbage bag. Is this what God had in mind for sex?

How else could Satan best destroy the human race? I believe that his best strategy would be to wreak havoc on marriage and its sanctity. Attacking marriage, the foundation of the family, damages humanity in all the ways we've contemplated and more. Marriage was the very first institution God set in place in our world. Before the commandments, before the church, before every other religious institution, God created marriage. He created marriage as a union for us here on earth, and the very next day He rested, thus creating a remembrance and reflection of His work on our behalf and establishing our union with and marriage to Him.

When you get married, you establish a partnership with your mate. You decide that you will take on this world together, whatever suffering and joy it may bring. God knew that two was better than one. Whereas one might meet suffering and crumble, two could stand together. God knew that it would take the two of you to join forces and remain loyal not only to one another but also to the children that could be born from that love and loyalty. When the foundation of marriage is strong, the family can prosper. Families are the check-and-balance system of our world. There is no love or loyalty quite like that of a family. Families can hold each other accountable and together.

The world would have you forget how powerful the union of marriage is. Marriage may still be fashionable, but "till death do us part" isn't. Loyalty is no longer a virtue in this individualistic society. The media would have you believe that marriage and monogamy is old-fashioned and outdated. Maybe if we spice it up—allow for multiple partners within marriage, petition our government for the right for same-sex couples to get married, divorce because we found someone else who gets whatever we're going through right now a little better than our spouse does—perhaps that would make marriage "cool" in the twenty-first century. Satan is out to destroy marriage, and the funny thing is, most of America doesn't even realize it. In fact, we're helping him!

Satan has coerced us into accepting ideas that are completely contradictory to the Bible on the pretext of loving and accepting one another, i.e., society tells us we're bigots if we don't accept homosexuality, and society says we are old-fashioned if we can't be open-minded about other people's sexual preferences and/or multiple partners. We stopped reading the Bible for ourselves and allowed others to tell us what they think it means. The Bible never condones sin, though. Love the sinner, yes. But let's be clear on this: sin separates us from God, and our only chance at salvation is to be connected to God, not separated. Satan doesn't want us to think about that.

Marriage has the power to give the greatest glory to God imaginable and to produce righteous children who will bring light to a world of darkness. Marriage is sacred, and Satan is like a wild dog foaming at the mouth to sever its bonds. Satan wants you to believe that sex is one thing and marriage is another, and family is yet again another—all separate entities. But they are all related, they are all interconnected. Taking away the reverence for sex helps destroy the sanctity of marriage not only for this generation but also for the generations to come.

My father has told me on countless occasions that a world containing only corrupted children is a world that grace can no longer reach. Once the purity and innocence of children is infiltrated, Satan will have free rein and will try to reestablish himself as king of this earth, because without good seed, what can be grown? Your marriage is your child's best chance at prosperity.

Focus on the Family published an article for Christian singles by Shana Schutte in which she drew inspiration from a few other writers about true intimacy.[8] One of them, Donald Joy, wrote an article for *Christianity Today* that referenced a study of 100,000 women that linked "early sexual experience with dissatisfaction in their present marriages, unhappiness with the level of sexual intimacy and the prevalence of low self-esteem." Another of the writers, Alice Fryling, said: "Genital sex is an expression of intimacy, not the means to intimacy. True intimacy springs from verbal and emotional communion. True intimacy is built on a commitment to honesty, love, and freedom. True intimacy is not primarily a sexual encounter. Intimacy, in fact, has almost nothing to do with our sex organs. A prostitute may expose her body, but her relationships are hardly intimate."

I tell my students every semester that communication research shows that the most fulfilling means of intimacy is not through sex, but through self-disclosure. By self-disclosure I mean sharing your personal thoughts, dreams, beliefs, and goals with another person. If you want to experience intimacy, connect with your dating partner through self-disclosure. This will create a bond that is hard to sever, because men typically do not self-disclose. If a woman can get a man to connect with her mentally, she will have his undivided attention. Usually a man shares his thoughts, dreams, and goals with only his mother.

Men base their friendships not on connectedness and self-disclosure but on shared activities. They are best friends because they both love basketball or they both go fishing or they run or bike together. Women, however, base their friendships on connectedness and self-disclosure. Women know how to communicate and get their feelings across. Women are nurturing, loving creatures—it's simply what they do best. Far too many women are making the mistake of using sex to create intimacy and are brokenhearted when it doesn't work. It doesn't work because if you want to create a bond through sex, it can be done only when coupled with deep connectedness and self-disclosure—and that, my friends, is called marriage.

Galatians 6:7, 8 says: "Do not be deceived: God cannot be mocked. A man reaps what he sows. Whoever sows to please their flesh, from the flesh will reap destruction; whoever sows to please the Spirit, from the Spirit will reap eternal life." So where does this text leave us? If most of you reading this have already had sex, how in the world do you start this thing over? Guess what, if God didn't forgive sin, we would all be in serious trouble. But 1 John 1:9 says: "If we confess our sins, he is faithful and just and will forgive us our sins and purify us from all unrighteousness."

Psalm 103:12 tells us what happens when we repent of our sins; God removes them from His memory.: "As far as the east is from the west, so far has he removed our transgressions from us."

Your sins are what have separated you from God, but through the crucifixion Jesus has provided restoration and healing. I don't know about you, but you can find me at the foot of the cross.

Response to Critic Number Five

Claim: *Virgin* is another word for *loser*.

Reply: When I finally meet the person of my dreams and I get to tell them on our wedding night that I loved them before I knew them, and that because of that, I have saved myself for this moment to experience this incredible act with only them for the rest of my life, I'm pretty sure a lot of words may come to their mind. Honestly, I don't think *loser* will be one of them.

---

[1] www.fabaudrey.com/quotes.

[2] Bonnie Rochman, "Sex and Self-esteem: A Big Boost for Men, Not So Much for Women," *Time*, May 9, 2011.

[3] www.barna.org/culture-articles/144-a-new-generation-of-adults-bends-moral-and-sexual-rules-to-their-liking.

[4] www.cdc.gov/std/stats10/adol.htm.

[5] www.psychologytoday.com/blog/co-parenting-after-divorce/201205/father-absence-father-deficit-father-hunger.

[6] Abraham Swamidoss, "Father's Day Cards," *Lake Union Herald*, June 2012.

[7] www.cdc.gov/reproductivehealth/data_stats/Abortion.htm.

[8] www.focusonthefamily.com/faith/christian_singles/being_single_and_faithful/three_lies_about_sex_before_marriage.aspx.

Chapter 6

If God Is Real, Then He Is Homophobic

"In reality, there are no biblical literalists, only selective literalists. By abolishing slavery and ordaining women, millions of Protestants have gone far beyond biblical literalism. It's time we did the same for homophobia."
—William Sloane Coffin, American clergyman and peace activist[1]

The debate between Christians and secularists on the topic of homosexuality has been intense. I mentioned earlier that 60 percent of young people are leaving the church. There are various reasons they leave their pews, one of them being that God is presented as being far too exclusive. It cannot be denied that moral attitudes are changing, opinions have many shades of gray, and formerly well-defined lines are blurry. Before you assume that you know what I am about to say about the biblical truth concerning homosexuality, I ask that you read this chapter in its entirety.

It is no secret to anyone who knows me that I love gay people. I don't know what it is about me, but since elementary school I have been naturally drawn to the gay kid in the class. Perhaps I noticed they didn't quite fit in, and that appeals to me, because for a long time I always felt like the misfit of every group. There were many days during my childhood I sat alone or ate alone because I just didn't fit in with the rest of my class. I have always marched to the beat of my own drum. So when I see someone else who may be a little bit different, I tend to feel connected. There have been many evenings I went to dinner and was the only female at a table full of men. One might have assumed I was quite popular with the fellas, but in truth, they were all gay.

I also became very good friends with a girl at my work. I didn't know it when we started having our lunches together, but I found out within a few months that she was gay. She had been engaged to a man and called off the wedding. I could relate to this since I had been engaged before and called it off as well. I was shocked when she told me later that she called off the wedding because she was a lesbian and didn't want to drag someone she cared about into this firestorm that was going on inside her heart. She was very distraught, and I felt for her. She needed a friend, and I wanted to be one. I love gay people, mainly because I have learned to genuinely love *people*.

I think this is a confusing issue, because at this point in world history everyone probably knows someone who is a homosexual. Someone we are close to tells us they are gay, and we don't know how to rectify what we know the Bible says and how we feel for this person. Because this is difficult, we often tell them what they want to hear in an attempt to keep the relationship. We love them, and so we feel we have no choice.

Ed Dobson, former vice president of the Moral Majority, said this: "I haven't changed in the sense that I believe sexuality is a gift from God to be expressed exclusively within the commitment of heterosexual marriage and that all other expressions of that are outside the boundaries of God's creative intent as revealed in the Scripture. However, I do not believe that gives you a license to hate people, including homosexuals, and I think part of the struggle for people is that it's easy, it's easy to beat up what you don't understand. I have sat and listened to story after story after story from gay people of their journey and have cried with them and tried to listen to the awful pain they go through. [It] hasn't changed what I believe about the practice of homosexuality, but it has reminded me that 'whom you would change you must first love.' Martin Luther King, Jr., said that. And in general, Christians have not been very good about loving gay people. Oh, they'll tell you they hate the sin but they love the sinner, but I don't see much love for the sinner."[2]

I love what Martin Luther King, Jr., said: "Whom you would change, you must first love." I agree with that statement completely. But here's the thing: if you love them, you also have a duty and responsibility to be honest with them and honest with yourself. I love my gay friends dearly, but I will never condone their behavior. I love my heterosexual friends who participate in partying, drinking, and sleeping around; I love them dearly, but I cannot and will not condone their behavior. I can't because if I go against what I know to be true in an attempt to make them feel I am not judging them, I am failing them in the long run.

Rick Warren, a pastor most popular for his book *The Purpose Driven Life*, said this: "Our culture has accepted two huge lies. The first is that if you disagree with someone's lifestyle, you must fear or hate them. The second is that to love someone means you agree with everything they believe or do. Both are nonsense. You don't have to compromise convictions to be compassionate."

I have two rules when it comes to talking with my friends about my views on sexuality. Rule number one: I never give advice they did not ask me for. If they don't want my opinion, I don't give it to them. They know I am a Christian, they know I am extremely committed to my relationship with Christ, and they know I am extremely opinionated. But just as I don't force God onto people who are not asking me about Him, I don't force my convictions about sexuality on them either. We have a relationship, so more times than not they will eventually ask me what my opinion is on their practices. You see, typically, that eventually they will seek out my opinion without me forcing it on them, because generally people don't care what you know until they know that you care. That is when my second rule comes into play.

Rule number two: Always speak the truth. Don't hide out of fear, don't tell them what they want to hear, and don't sweep it under the rug and hope no one notices. If they ask me for my counsel, I am honest in my feedback.

I believe that practicing homosexuality is a sin. I also believe that Satan is using homosexuality brilliantly. He knows the act of same-sex sexual encounters is appalling to Christ, so he is using it to destroy sex, families, and relationships—and all in the name of love. Satan wants you to think that love means acceptance, but it doesn't. Christ loves you unconditionally, but you'll never catch Him excusing any of your bad behavior because He doesn't want to offend you. He cannot do that because there is simply too much at stake.

I am sure that people will disagree with my position. I am sure that some people may close this book right now because I'm not saying what they want to hear. But I assure you that I am not one of those people who simply says, "I have friends who are gay," and really mean I met a guy on a train once who was gay and seemed nice. I have many friends who are homosexual who are bright spots in my life. They love me, and I love them. My heart aches when they explain the mental conflict they often go through. I pray with them, and when I am alone, I keep good on my promises to continue in prayer for them. Their plight is not lost on me. I do love gay people, but that doesn't mean that I condone the practice of homosexuality.

This is how I have come to believe what I believe:

Leviticus 20:13 says: "If a man has sexual relations with a man as one does with a woman, both of them have done what is detestable. They are to be put to death; their blood will be on their own heads."

I'm not sure how much clearer our understanding of what God thinks about this specific sin could get. He views it as He views all sin: detestable. And here is what Romans 1:21-32 says about what happens when we give up God to fulfill the appetites of our carnal, sinful nature:

"For although they knew God, they neither glorified him as God nor gave thanks to him, but their thinking became futile and their foolish hearts were darkened. Although they claimed to be wise, they became fools and exchanged the glory of the immortal God for images made to look like a mortal human being and birds and animals and reptiles.

"Therefore God gave them over in the sinful desires of their hearts to sexual impurity for the degrading of their bodies with one another. They exchanged the truth about God for a lie, and worshiped and served created things rather than the Creator—who is forever praised. Amen.

"Because of this, God gave them over to shameful lusts. Even their women exchanged natural sexual relations for unnatural ones. In the same way the men also abandoned natural relations with women and were inflamed with lust for one another. Men committed shameful acts with other men, and received in themselves the due penalty for their error.

"Furthermore, just as they did not think it worthwhile to retain the knowledge of God, so God gave them over to a depraved mind, so that they do what ought not to be done. They have become filled with every kind of wickedness, evil, greed and depravity. They are full of envy, murder, strife, deceit and malice. They are gossips, slanderers, God-haters, insolent, arrogant and boastful; they invent ways of doing evil; they disobey their parents; they have no understanding, no fidelity, no love, no mercy. Although they know God's righteous decree that those who do such things deserve death, they not only continue to do these very things but also approve of those who practice them."

In Jude 7 we are reminded of what happened at Sodom and Gomorrah: "In a similar way, Sodom and Gomorrah and the surrounding towns gave themselves up to sexual immorality and perversion. They serve as an example of those who suffer the punishment of eternal fire."

And in Proverbs 10:16, 17 we see we have a duty to admit sin when we see it: "The wages of the righteous is life, but the earnings of the wicked are sin and death. Whoever heeds discipline shows the way to life, but whoever ignores correction leads others astray."

The world wants us to think that in order to love homosexuals, we have to accept their practice. So Satan twists what the Bible says and tells us that if we don't condone their sin, we do not effectively love them as Christians are instructed to do. In other words, we must accept homosexuals as they are in order to be good disciples of God. If we do not accept the sin, we are infringing on their rights and are essentially bad Christians. This is why Satan cannot be marginalized. We cannot forget that this is Lucifer, who was one of the highest beings God created. Before he was the devil, he was a remarkable student. He knows all about how God feels about love. Just as he attempted to twist the words of the Bible when tempting Christ, he is twisting Christian ideas and concepts now. Same tactic, different situation.

It's easy to see the divide Satan is causing in our churches with this issue, especially among our young people. No one wants to stand up for what's right anymore; we want to be politically correct. Instead of denying sin, we would rather deny God. I know many good Christians who are condoning the practice of homosexuality; some of these Christians are studying in our seminary. This honestly scares me. With some issues in the Bible there are differences in translations or simply not many applicable scriptures available, so I can see confusion setting in. This, however, is not one of those topics. With this topic we can't handle the pressure society is putting on us, we don't want to appear too conservative, and so we ignore the Bible's teachings in an attempt to remain popular. Christ was not popular, and He was very clear that if they rejected Him, the world would also reject those who stand for Him.

John 15:18 says, "If the world hates you, keep in mind that it hated me first." They killed Him. He called them out on their dishonesty, He was clear on their misunderstandings of Scripture, He didn't make excuses for bad behavior, and so rather than accept His offers of redemption, they killed Him. They wanted to shut Him up so that they could go on doing things their way. And so on a cross He died, killed by the very people He came to save. And I would venture to say that if He were to come again and be among us on earth, we would kill Him again, because if your heart is with the world, you will do anything to keep it, even if it means rejecting the Son of God.

Let's take spirituality out of it. Let's focus instead on the data. Is homosexuality a healthy lifestyle? In the book *Why We Whisper*, put together by U.S. Senator Jim DeMint and J. David Woodard, Ph.D., the authors explore the health risks of homosexual sex.

"John R. Diggs, Jr., M.D., in his report *The Health Risks of Gay Sex*, compiles dozens of studies over several decades. He concludes that the medical and social science evidence indicate that homosexual behavior is uniformly unhealthy.

"'Homosexuals, though probably less than two percent of the population, account for the bulk of cases of syphilis, gonorrhea, hepatitis B, the gay bowel syndrome, tuberculosis, cytomegalovirus, and HIV. Homosexuals also experience a high rate of anal cancer, incontinence, parasitic and other intestinal infections, hepatitis A, and cervical cancer.

"'High levels of promiscuity among homosexuals exacerbate the spread of STDs and other health problems. One study found 75 percent of white gay males claimed to have had more than 100 lifetime male sex partners; 15 percent claimed 100-249 sex partners; seventeen claimed 250-499; fifteen claimed 500-999; and twenty-eight claimed more than 1,000 lifetime male sex partners. . . .

"'Homosexuals, on average, lose twenty years of life expectancy. The probability of a twenty-year-old gay or bisexual man living to sixty-five years was only 32 percent, compared to 78 percent of men in general. . . .

"'Long-term sexual fidelity is rare in gay, lesbian, and bisexual (GLB) relationships. One study reported that 66 percent of gay couples reported sex outside the relationship within the first year, and nearly 90 percent if the relationship lasted five years.'"[3]

Even without the spiritual implications, homosexuality is a serious health concern. C. Everett Koop, M.D., former U.S. surgeon general, said: "When you have sex with someone, you are having sex with everyone they have had sex with for the past 10 years, and everyone they and their partners have had sex with for the past 10 years."

Without a doubt homosexuality is an unhealthy lifestyle. The statistics are in, and just like heterosexual promiscuity, homosexuality causes severe health issues. Even when the theological issues are removed, we should be able to see the red flags surrounding this lifestyle. When God says not to do something, He has a reason for it. He knows how harmful it is to our health because He knows how He designed us to operate. DeMint and Woodard also have this to say:

"The most serious and fastest growing STD cases are among men who have sex with men (MSM). This group carries two thirds of HIV infections (even though less than 5 percent of males say they are homosexual), and of those who have the disease, about 25 percent don't know they have it. When direct and indirect costs are considered, HIV/AIDS cases account for nearly half of the total costs associated with STDs. Cases of rectal chlamydia, gonorrhea, and syphilis are also increasing at alarming rates among the MSM group. 'The syphilis rate among U.S. men soared

81 percent between 2000 and 2004, primarily as a result of increases in reported cases among homosexual males.' . . .

"Every American pays a high price for STDs as a result of a cultural preoccupation with sexual freedom. Taxes are higher and health insurance costs more for everyone. American productivity is lower, and our economic future is diminished. The lifetime medical cost for just one HIV patient is approximately $200,000. One study of patients receiving care for HIV found that 47 percent were paid for by the government programs Medicaid or Medicare, 33 percent had private insurance (which makes insurance more expensive for everyone) and 20 percent were uninsured (which shifts the cost of health care to those who pay). STDs create secondhand consequences for all Americans.[4]

In 2000 the Centers for Disease Control and Prevention (CDC) estimated more than 65 million Americans have incurable sexually transmitted diseases.[5] Still, few are willing even to whisper that sex outside of marriage might be both harmful *and* wrong for individuals and the country. People may have the *right* to have sex outside of marriage, but is it right to ask others to pay for the consequences?

This is the truth about the effect of homosexuality on health. Homosexuality is unhealthy and unbiblical. It is a practice that goes against God's design. The practice of homosexuality is a sin, and sin is immoral. But you don't change sinners through hatred; you change sinners by introducing them to a love that is just so powerful it cannot be ignored. I stopped serving God out of fear a long time ago. Now I serve God because I am in awe of what He has done for me in spite of who I am. When you fall in love with someone, hurting them hurts you.

No sin is beyond God's plan of salvation. God did not give up His life to save only a certain type of sinner who commits certain types of sin. God came to this world to save everyone who would accept His gift. The plan is simple: "Seek the Lord while he may be found; call on him while he is near. Let the wicked forsake their ways and the unrighteous their thoughts. Let them turn to the Lord, and he will have mercy on them, and to our God, for he will freely pardon" (Isaiah 55:6, 7).

Satan wants to make things more complicated. He wants to blur the lines and confuse our thoughts. Don't let him do it. Read the Bible for yourself. Meet Christ for yourself and stand for Him out of pure loyalty. Love the sinner; hate the sin. But this time, actually love the sinner.

Response to Critic Number Six

Claim: If God is real, then He is homophobic.

Reply: If you read the Bible, you won't find that God singles out gays and bashes them. God does not hate gays; what He hates is sin. He hates sexual promiscuity, greed, deceit, murder, blasphemy, disrespect, and a long list of other practices that hurt human beings. He loves us so much that He died for us *because* of our sinfulness, hoping that through His death we will learn to reject sin and choose life.

---

[1] www.religioustolerance.org/homquote.htm.

[2] *Ibid.*

[3] Jim DeMint and J. David Woodard, Ph.D., *Why We Whisper* (Lanham, Md.: Rowman & Littlefield Pub., Inc., 2008), pp. 142, 143.

[4] *Ibid.*, pp. 130, 131.

[5] www.cdc.gov/std/trends2000/trends2000.pdf.

Chapter 7

If God Is Real, Then He Is All About Hell, Judgment, and Punishment

"The belief of a cruel God makes a cruel man."
—Thomas Paine, author, activist, and revolutionary[1]

One of the biggest problems atheists have with Christianity involves the question "Why would anyone want to serve such a vengeful, mean God?"

In the Old Testament the tough side of God comes across loud and clear, and some of us don't like what we see. Some simply disregard Him altogether while others were taught to love Him, so this picture of God may cause them to serve Him out of fear. The biggest mistake people make with the Bible, though, is not reading it in its entirety. We take pieces here and bits there, and we put together our own picture of God. But this gives us an incomplete view of Him.

There have been times that I've looked at God's actions in the Bible and thought, *That was harsh*. I've even felt that at certain times in the Old Testament, God was angry. I saw Him rebuke people or nations and send the Israelites out to destroy entire people groups, and I couldn't help seeing God as a strict executor of punishment. However, the second time I read through the Bible, I caught something I had missed the first time. I realized the significance of the story of Rahab within the larger story of the battle of Jericho, and for the first time I fully understood the workings of God in regard to punishment.

The battle of Jericho was Joshua's first battle as leader of the Israelites after Moses' death. The story begins in Joshua 2 with Joshua sending out two men to spy on Jericho.

"Then Joshua son of Nun secretly sent two spies from Shittim. 'Go, look over the land,' he said, 'especially Jericho.' So they went and entered the house of a prostitute named Rahab and stayed there" (verse 1).

Shortly after the spies go inside Rahab's house, someone alerts the king of Jericho that the two men are inside their walls.

"The king of Jericho was told, 'Look, some of the Israelites have come here tonight to spy out the land.' So the king of Jericho sent this message to Rahab: 'Bring out the men who came to you and entered your house, because they have come to spy out the whole land'" (verses 2, 3).

Here we see Rahab do something interesting: betray her own people.

"But the woman had taken the two men and hidden them. She said, 'Yes, the men came to me, but I did not know where they had come from. At dusk, when it was time to close the city gate, they left. I don't know which way they went. Go after them quickly. You may catch up with them.' (But she had taken them up to the roof and hidden them under the stalks of flax she had laid out on the roof.) So the men set out in pursuit of the spies on the road that leads to the fords of the Jordan, and as soon as the pursuers had gone out, the gate was shut" (verses 4-7).

This action on Rahab's part is powerful enough on its own, but what she does next is downright remarkable. This woman of Jericho, this prostitute, this traitor to her country, recognizes something profound. Sometime between meeting the spies and providing refuge to them in her house, Rahab puts her faith in Yahweh.

"Before the spies lay down for the night, she went up on the roof and said to them, 'I know that the Lord has given you this land and that a great fear of you has fallen on us, so that all who live in this country are melting in fear because of you. We have heard how the Lord dried up the water of the Red Sea for you when you came out of Egypt, and what you did to Sihon and Og, the two kings of the Amorites east of the Jordan, whom you completely destroyed. When we heard of it, our hearts melted in fear and everyone's courage failed because of you, for the Lord your God is God in heaven above and on the earth below'" (verses 8-11).

Here we see Rahab recognize and confess that the God of the Hebrews is the God of the universe. Her next words help us understand the importance of coming to God in our times of trouble. After she confesses that God is the only God, she asks for His protection for herself and then unselfishly begs protection for those she loves as well.

" 'Now then, please swear to me by the Lord that you will show kindness to my family, because I have shown kindness to you. Give me a sure sign that you will spare the lives of my father and mother, my brothers and sisters, and all who belong to them—and that you will save us from death.' 'Our lives for your lives!' the men assured her. 'If you don't tell what we are doing, we will treat you kindly and faithfully when the Lord gives us the land'" (verses 12-14).

The spies tell Rahab to mark her home with a scarlet cord so that she, along with anyone else in her house, will be spared when Jericho is destroyed (verses 17-21). Joshua 6 concludes the story, and as you will recall, the walls of Jericho came tumbling down when the trumpets sounded and the Israelites shouted. Rahab's house was built into the wall of Jericho, and when the walls of Jericho collapsed, that one part of the wall—the section with a small scarlet cord in a window—stayed upright. The two spies were not the only ones who heard Rahab's confession of faith in Yahweh; the Lord of lords heard it as well. Before Joshua had his men burn the city to the ground, he sent men to bring out Rahab and her family, who were allowed to live among the Israelites thereafter.

This story tells me that God is a God of mercy. A vengeful God would have destroyed Rahab along with everyone else in Jericho. Although she never knew it, Rahab became one of Jesus' ancestors.

This story of Rahab is an instance in which we get to see what happened behind the scenes. I think of other stories in which God destroyed entire cities and left nothing but rubble. I can't see behind the scenes, but God can. He is eager to save as many people as will let Him, even a prostitute who calls on His name. He would have spared Sodom and Gomorrah if, as Abraham bargained, 10 people with good in their hearts could have been found within their gates. There weren't 10, but God saved all the people who would allow Him to (see Genesis 18; 19). And we read in Jonah that God gave the wicked people of Nineveh a chance to repent, and when they did, He saved them. This is why I can take God at His word when He says in Ezekiel 18:23, "Do I take any pleasure in the death of the wicked? declares the Sovereign Lord. Rather, am I not pleased when they turn from their ways and live?"

It is too late for Satan, so now he is trying to convince you that God is vengeful and hateful because he has been barred from heaven. But look what Satan has done. Since being expelled from heaven, he has sadistically tormented all of humanity because God loves us so much. Every disease, every murder, every lie, every depraved act, has been orchestrated by Satan. The being who once stood by the throne of God, face to face with goodness and glory, has poured out utter malice and destruction on our world. God knows the universe cannot permanently endure the existence of such a being, and so he must be destroyed. But Satan's sentence doesn't have to be yours.

Ellen White writes: "Satan is constantly at work, with intense energy and under a thousand disguises, to misrepresent the character and government of God. With extensive, well-organized plans and marvelous power, he is working to hold the inhabitants of the world under his deceptions. God, the One infinite and all-wise, sees the end from the beginning, and in dealing with evil His plans were far-reaching and comprehensive. It was His purpose, not merely to put down the rebellion, but to demonstrate to all the universe the nature of the rebellion. God's plan was unfolding, showing both His justice and His mercy, and fully vindicating His wisdom and righteousness in His dealings with evil."[2]

We have to remember that God also had to make extremely clear to the angels what Satan would have done had he not been cast out of heaven. As Lucifer, Satan had been their leader. And I am sure that when he began his rebellion, he didn't start by trying to kill God the Son. Sin is almost never that dramatic. It is enticing because it moves slowly, and before you know it, you are stuck somewhere you thought you'd never be, doing things you never thought you'd do. The plan of salvation, ultimately designed to save humanity, was also a chance for the angels to see how far Satan would go if God did not destroy him. I am sure they were shocked as they watched Satan's rebellion unfold.

White continues: "The holy inhabitants of other worlds were watching with the deepest interest the events taking place on the earth. In the condition of the world that existed before the Flood they saw illustrated the results of the administration which Lucifer had endeavored to establish in heaven, in rejecting the authority of Christ and casting aside the law of God. In those high-handed sinners of the antediluvian world they saw the subjects over whom Satan held sway. The thoughts of men's hearts were only evil continually (Genesis 6:5). Every emotion, every impulse and imagination, was at war with the divine principles of purity and peace and love. It was an example of the awful depravity resulting from Satan's policy to remove from God's creatures the restraint of His holy law."[3]

Adding insult to injury, the one who made sure that sin rotted this earth is blaming God for his own actions. Some of us have taken the bait. How agonizing it must be to be Jesus, to watch the world for which you gave your life continue to reject you, blame you for everything that causes them pain, and persistently trust the enemy over the friend.

It was while reading Ellen White's book *Early Writings* that I think I was able to truly understand what Jesus did when He developed the plan of salvation. Consequently, it is also one of my favorite books by White. If you are trying to think of a good place to start reading her work, I would suggest *Early Writings*. The background information it provides is powerful, and its descriptions of the end of time will tug right on your heartstrings because it doesn't take a scholar to recognize that the time she refers to is now.

In *Early Writings* White explains that after Adam sinned, heaven was filled with sorrow. They knew that humanity would be lost, and it pained them deeply. The angels had communicated with Adam and Eve often before the Fall. They had told them all about Satan and had warned them not to leave each other's side.[4] The angels knew that Adam and Eve had a better chance at evading Satan's temptations together then they did alone. To me, this is a huge nod to marriage: two are stronger than one.

Eve's first error was separating from her husband after she had been warned not to do so. I imagine it was curiosity that led her to wander off and that it was no mistake that she found herself at the forbidden tree. The fact that she found herself alone next to the only thing in the garden God Himself had already told her not to eat of goes to show that she was probably curious about this tree and may have gone alone on purpose. *Why would God not want us to eat of it?* she probably wondered. Warning: what starts as harmless curiosity may, in fact, destroy you. Give the devil an inch, and he will take a mile.

We all know what happened next. First Eve was disarmed by the intelligence of the serpent and amazed that it could talk. Once Satan had her ear, he executed his plan fully. He told her that God did not mean it when He said they would die; basically, God was just holding out on them. Eve became jealous that God would hold back something that would enlighten them, so she ate the fruit and then brought it to her husband.

White says that Adam was certain the serpent Eve spoke of was the devil they'd been warned against. He was afraid and saddened that his wife had just disobeyed God.[5] And then he did what many of us do—he picked the girl over God. He panicked at the thought of life without Eve, so he ate the fruit, thus choosing his earthly relationship over his heavenly one. We need to be very careful that no human relationship ever separates us from God. God is clear that our relationship with Him must be the most important relationship we have. If we spend hours with our girlfriend or boyfriend but give God only 30 minutes in the morning, it would be easy for us to fall into the same trap Adam did.

Adam spent the rest of his life regretting what he had done. White writes in *Patriarchs and Prophets* that when Adam and Eve saw the first flower die, they mourned for that flower more than we mourn the death of a loved one.[6] They had never seen death, and Adam knew the death of that plant was caused by his error. Every sick child, every death, every tear, was a reaction to his action in Eden. Adam grieved daily. Adam's death occurred, not because God was angry, but because God is merciful. He does not allow us to experience the awfulness of sin for eternity.

White says that Satan thought he had won after he caused sin in Eden. God had never let anyone die before. Satan himself was still alive and breathing after rebellion, so Satan thought that he had singlehandedly caused sin to exist perpetually.[7] If sin was to exist perpetually on earth, then earth would be his kingdom and he could reign in opposition to God forever. But God had a plan.

White writes: "I saw the lovely Jesus and beheld an expression of sympathy and sorrow upon His countenance. Soon I saw Him approach the exceeding bright light which enshrouded the Father. Said my accompanying angel, He is in close converse with His Father. The anxiety of the angels seemed to be intense while Jesus was communing with His Father. Three times He was shut in by the glorious light about the Father, and the third time He came from the Father, His person could be seen. His countenance was calm, free from all perplexity and doubt, and shone with benevolence and loveliness such as words cannot express. He then made known to the angelic host that a way of escape had been made for lost man. He told them that He had been pleading with His Father, and had offered to give His life a ransom, to take the sentence of death upon Himself, that through Him man might find pardon; that through the merits of His blood, and obedience to the law of God, they could have the favor of God, and be brought into the beautiful garden, and eat of the fruit of the tree of life."[8]

The angels were astonished at the plan of salvation. The thought of the perfect Son of God entering an imperfect world to be subjected to Satan's torment and ultimately dying to save humanity was overwhelming. The angels begged Jesus to let one of them take His place. Jesus explained to them that only His life would be a sufficient sacrifice and that His death would save many souls. He also told them that they would be assigned a great work. They would help Him at certain times during His ministry on earth.[9] When I read that, I was awed.

I love how sweet and kind and merciful my Savior is. The fact that someone would call this same Jesus cruel and vengeful is almost laughable. Here is what takes the cake for me:

"Satan still hoped that the great plan of salvation would fail. He exerted all his power to make the hearts of the people hard and their feelings bitter against Jesus. He hoped that so few would receive Him as the Son of God that He would consider His sufferings and sacrifice too great to make for so small a company. But I saw that if there had been but two who would have accepted Jesus as the Son of God and believed on Him to the saving of their souls, He would have carried out the plan."[10]

If there had been but two, even just you and me, Jesus would have paid the same price. Christ's love for us defies quantity, it defies logic, it defies any earthly love, and it defies even our own understanding. Jesus wants nothing more than to reunite us with God. He loves us intensely, but Satan is busy working to get us to reject Him so that the price He paid will not cover us. Don't let Satan win that battle. Don't let him convince you or your family or your neighbors that his lies about God are the truth. See to it that everyone you love is in heaven. If we all took more responsibility for the souls of the ones we love, Satan would not have as many followers.

God hates sin. He is literally in agony over this sin-sick world. If God was all about hellfire, judgment, and punishment, this world would already be over. The moment sin entered Eden He would have wiped us out, plain and simple. On the contrary, He put Himself smack-dab in the middle of the very thing He hates most. He became human and gave the ultimate sacrifice to save us. Only the intelligence of one of the highest created beings could distort this picture of love into that of an angry, vengeful God bent on destruction. You can see the devil's fingerprints all over that image.

Satan knows his days are numbered. He knows God will not excuse his rebellion, so he spends every single day trying to convince people that God's love and justice is actually anger and spitefulness. He wants you to accept the sentence he was given because misery loves company. However, if you are still breathing, God allows repentance. God is not done with your trial. He is your expert defense lawyer, and He is also your judge. If you lose this case, it's not because He wanted you to, but because you didn't care enough to show up.

Response to Critic Number Seven

Claim: If God is real, then He is all about hell, judgment, and punishment.

Reply: Jesus would have put Himself through the agony of crucifixion and dying for sin even if there had been only two sinners (or even just one). My God is a God of love and mercy. His mission since sin entered the world has been to save humans, not destroy them.

---

[1] Thomas Paine, "A Letter: Being an Answer to a Friend, on the Publication of *The Age of Reason*, Paris, May 12, 1797," *The Age of Reason* (Boston: J. P. Mendum, 1852), p. 205.

[2] E. G. White, *Patriarchs and Prophets*, p. 78.

[3] *Ibid.*, pp. 78, 79.

[4] Ellen G. White, *Early Writings* (Mountain View, Calif.: Pacific Press Pub. Assn., 1882), pp. 147, 148.

[5] *Ibid.*, p. 148.

[6] E. G. White, *Patriarchs and Prophets*, p. 62.

[7] E. G. White, *Early Writings*, p. 148.

[8] *Ibid.*, p. 149.

[9] *Ibid.*, pp. 150, 151.

[10] *Ibid.*, p. 159.

Chapter 8

If There Is a Day to Worship, It's Sunday

"You may read the Bible from Genesis to Revelation, and you will not find a single line authorizing the sanctification of Sunday. The Scriptures enforce the religious observance of Saturday, a day which we [the Roman Catholic Church] never sanctify."
—James Cardinal Gibbons[1]

I am a Seventh-day Adventist. I am a Seventh-day Adventist not just because my parents raised me as an Adventist, but because they also always encouraged me never to take anyone else's word for it. "Figure out everything for yourself," my dad always told me.

I never really had any qualms about the Sabbath. I grew up reading the Bible for myself, and I never read one sentence that caused me to think that Saturday, or the seventh day of the week, was not the Sabbath. Eventually I left my Adventist bubble and found myself in a secular high school. It was there that I was first introduced to people who worshipped on Sunday.

This adjustment did not really bother me. I was never attacked for worshiping on Saturday, because everyone in my small town knew families who did, even if they didn't. It wasn't bizarre to worship on Saturday, so I suppose that although I left the inner layers of my bubble, I was still cushioned.

During my freshman year of college, however, my bubble popped. I attended a Christian, but non-Adventist, college. I met many people who *did* care that I worshipped on Saturday. It was a harsh surprise to find out that because I kept the seventh-day Sabbath, I was somewhat of an outcast. I suppose the root of the problem was that when people asked why I went to church on Sabbath, I tried to cautiously soften the blow by explaining that my church kept a more literal understanding of Scripture. I thought this was being polite. At least it sounded better than "Because the Bible says we should."

Sometimes the conversation ended there, but other times it didn't. The individual would ask what I meant, and I would explain that the Bible refers to the seventh day as the Sabbath on multiple occasions, and so we honor that.

The response was usually something to the effect of "So you're saying I am not honoring it?"

To which I would say something like "No, I am not saying that. I am saying my church follows the Bible more literally."

"So you're saying I am worshipping on the wrong day?"

"I am simply telling you which day I worship on and why because you asked."

People would take great offense to this, and eventually word spread across campus that I was an Adventist. Of course, no one knew what an Adventist was; they just knew that I was one and that I thought they all were wrong. At this point in my life I was not at all concerned with who was right and who was wrong. I did not care nor was I worried about which day of the week they worshipped on, so I didn't understand why they were so offended and concerned with which day I worshipped on.

Eventually the favorite Bible teacher on campus approached me after a class and asked me if I really was an Adventist. (No kidding, word really reached faculty!) I started feeling a bit nervous that I was going to get stuck in a discussion with him about why I worshipped on Sabbath.

"I keep the Sabbath too," he said. "I work on Sunday, but I rest on Sabbath. I have never known a group of people who knew their Bible as deeply as Adventists. I knew there was something special about you, kid." And he winked and sent me on my way. Now, I am not going to comment on his explanation of Sabbathkeeping, as that is his personal lifestyle and religious choice, but I was touched that he went out of his way to affirm me and my religion.

The reason people worship on Saturday? The Bible says to. E. Lonnie Melashenko said, "There was no question in the time of Christ and the apostles as to which day was the Sabbath."[2] So how did Saturday worship get switched to Sunday worship?

Melashenko's book *What the Bible Says About . . .* has been invaluable in my research, and many of the points that follow are covered in the chapter "The Change of the Sabbath." I highly recommend this book if you are looking for a quick read that will help you better understand what the Bible says about various doctrines.

Between A.D. 132 and 135 Jews found themselves under persecution by Rome after the Bar Kokhba revolt. A Jewish leader named Simon bar Kokhba, whom many Jews believed to be the Messiah, led the third major Jewish rebellion against the Romans. After the Romans crushed the rebellion, they barred the Jews from Jerusalem. Although the Christian Jews did not follow Bar Kokhba because they already knew Jesus Christ was the true Messiah, the Romans still barred every Jew, Christian or not, from Jerusalem. Christians became very sensitive to being identified with the Jews, and the seventh-day Sabbath was one of the identifiers that linked them with Judaism. In an effort to distance themselves from the Jews, Christians began minimizing the importance of Sabbathkeeping.

Also during this time many Christians who had formerly been sun worshippers began rationalizing that worshipping Christ on the first day of the week, the "sun day," would be an easier transition for other pagans. When Sunday first entered the Christian arena, it was simply a holiday, not necessarily a day of worship, and both days were kept in reverence for centuries. Because of paganism, and later persecution, Saturday worship became more and more marginalized.

In 321 Emperor Constantine declared that all government offices, courts, and shops were to be closed on the first day of the week, or the day of the sun. And in 364 the Council of Laodicea decreed that the church had changed the official day of worship from Saturday to Sunday.

Thousands of years earlier Daniel had written: "The ten horns are ten kings who will come from this kingdom. After them another king will arise, different from the earlier ones; he will subdue three kings. He will speak against the Most High and oppress his holy people and try to change the set times and the laws. The holy people will be delivered into his hands for a time, times and half a time" (Daniel 7:24, 25).

This prophecy about the changing of times refers to the changing of Sabbath observance from the seventh day to the first day. The fourth commandment is the only one of the Ten Commandments that has anything to do with a set time. This change was brought about by the Catholic Church, which they acknowledge and continue to assert that they, as the head church, have the power to do.[3]

So to be clear, the Bible never says anything about changing the Sabbath from the seventh day to the first day. So what happens now if, out of ignorance, many of us have been breaking the fourth commandment?

God is grace and mercy. Therefore, we can be assured that we will be held accountable only for what we know. Paul says in Romans 7:7 that we truly understand our sin when we understand the law: "What shall we say, then? Is the law sinful? Certainly not! Nevertheless, I would not have known what sin was had it not been for the law. For I would not have known what coveting really was if the law had not said, 'You shall not covet.'"

If you have been neglecting the seventh day for the first day of the week, or haven't really respected any day at all, you are warmly invited to meet God and worship Him this Sabbath. He doesn't care where you were last Sabbath, as long as you can join Him on this one.

Another error people often make is not acknowledging how important the Sabbath is. The Sabbath is the covenant between Creator and creation. If you think it's a nonfactor, you couldn't be more wrong. God finished creating on Friday, the sixth day of the week. He rested on the seventh day from all the work He had done. I would imagine that not only did He rest on the seventh day, but He also enjoyed the fruits of the other six days of His labor.

The crowning figure of His creation was humanity, which He created in His own image, and the Sabbath allowed time for humans to see everything that God had just made. Adam and Eve were experiencing so many incredible new things. I am sure they were filled with awe, love, and wonder as they explored Eden hand in hand, relishing the thought that life had just begun. God finished creating life on a Friday, then rested on Sabbath and enjoyed all that He had done. Thousands of years later, again on a Friday, Jesus prepared to observe the Sabbath as He hung on the cross. After His death for our sins, Christ rested on the seventh day of the week.

Loron Wade writes in his book *The Ten Commandments*:

"When the Lord gave the Ten Commandments at Sinai, He explained the reason for the Sabbath by pointing back to Creation. But when Moses repeated them 40 years later, He quoted them in a way that clearly foreshadowed the second reason: 'Remember that you were a slave in the land of Egypt, and the Lord your God brought you out of there by a mighty hand and by an outstretched arm; *therefore* the Lord your God commanded you to observe the sabbath day' (Deuteronomy 5:15, NASB).

"God created human beings to occupy a position of rulership (Genesis 1:26, 27). Slavery is the opposite of this. Not only had the Lord rescued His people from literal slavery, but it was His intention to restore them to their trust relationship with Him (Exodus 19:4), and as a result to a leadership position by elevating them to a 'royal priesthood' (see verses 5, 6; 1 Peter 2:9; Revelation 5:10). Thus the Sabbath is a celebration not only of Creation but also of redemption."[4]

Anyone who thinks that the instructions in God's Word are trivial, or don't matter, or are not important, are vastly disconnected from Scripture. If there is one thing I have learned through my own Bible study, it is how intentional, purposeful, and methodical God really is. He does not blow smoke, He does not require insignificant gestures, and He did not carelessly pluck a day of worship out of the sky. Once you understand how precise God is and how incredibly symbolic and genius His every word is, you will begin to truly understand His character.

We will never fully understand all of His work, but we can, out of respect, follow the requirements He has delineated clearly—the Ten Commandments, including the Sabbath commandment, being one set of instructions that were very clearly stated. To honestly think that the Ten Commandments—something Christ engraved in stone with His *finger*—are not important or shouldn't be followed precisely demonstrates a severe disconnect. To know God's character is to know His intentionality. Don't be fooled.

I love how God says, "Remember the Sabbath day by keeping it holy" (Exodus 20:8). He recognizes that this fourth commandment is going to be the only commandment that people will essentially forget. They will forget what Constantine and what the Council of Laodicea did in the 300s, and they will genuinely believe that the first day, the day of the sun, was to replace the seventh day, the Sabbath of the Lord your God. Without any scriptural evidence to support this substitution, the entire world will turn from seventh-day worship to first-day worship. Our loving Father reminds us, thousands of years before the switch even takes place, to remember the Sabbath and keep it holy because for six days the Lord labored, but on the seventh day He rested. The only commandment we have forgotten is the only commandment in which He said "remember." Ironic, isn't it?

Satan tricked Eve in the garden by insinuating that God did not mean exactly what He said in regard to the tree of knowledge of good and evil. Satan is really good at twisting words and making you question just how much God means what He says. For Eve, the consequences of disregarding God's instructions were deadly. When God speaks, we would do ourselves a service to listen.

Isaiah 66:22, 23 says that in the New Jerusalem, after Christ has conquered sin and vanquished death, the saved will worship on the Sabbath just as Adam and Eve did before the Fall: "'As the new heavens and the new earth that I make will endure before me,' declares the Lord, 'so will your name and descendants endure. From one New Moon to another and from one Sabbath to another, all mankind will come and bow down before me,' says the Lord."

Revelation 22:14 explains the necessity of Christians coming back to and following precisely all 10 commandments: "Blessed are those who do His commandments, that they may have the right to the tree of life, and may enter through the gates into the city" (NKJV). It was rebellion through sin that denied Adam and Eve from partaking of the tree of life in the garden, and only the people obedient to all of God's commandments will partake of the tree of life in the restored Eden when sin is no more.

I think it important to note here that I believe the six days of Creation were literal days. It blows my mind the number of Christians who have denounced the literal six-day creation. And how a Seventh-day Adventist Christian, who worships on the seventh-day Sabbath, does not believe that the world was created in six literal days is beyond me. Why exactly would a person worship on the seventh-day Sabbath then? God is clear in Exodus 20:11: "For in six days the Lord made the heavens and the earth, the sea, and all that is in them, but he rested on the seventh day. Therefore the Lord blessed the Sabbath day and made it holy." If a person does not believe God created the world in six literal days, it just doesn't make sense that he or she would keep holy the seventh literal day of the week.

Ellen White says this of Creation week: "But the assumption that the events of the first week required thousands upon thousands of years, strikes directly at the foundation of the fourth commandment. It represents the Creator as commanding men to observe the week of literal days in commemoration of vast, indefinite periods. This is unlike His method of dealing with His creatures. It makes indefinite and obscure that which He has made very plain. It is infidelity in its most insidious and hence most dangerous form; its real character is so disguised that it is held and taught by many who profess to believe the Bible."[5]

If you are so desperate to prove science that you must make dark what God has made clear, then your allegiance is already blurry. It is heartbreaking to see professed Bible followers questioning a six-day creation because it does not align with science. Guess what? When it comes to believing that Jesus Christ is God in human flesh and that He rose from the dead three days after His crucifixion, you are going to be hard pressed to correlate everything with science. At some point you just have to choose. You either follow God or follow humanity. You cannot have two masters.

The older I get and the more developed my personal relationship with Christ has become, the more emphasis I have placed on my Sabbath. I see how much the Sabbath is a benefit to my life. My husband is naturally a hard worker who borders on being a workaholic. When we purchased our first home, I was quite certain that if it were not for that mandated break from Friday sundown to Saturday sundown, I would never see him. I thought about families who do not have a Sabbath to force daddies inside from painting windows and pulling weeds, and it made my heart sink. My husband loves his family, but sometimes he gets tunnel vision on a project, and only the setting of the sun on Friday evening can snap him out of it. And praise God! Our family needs him, and the time we spend together every week trading in the sound of a television for the strumming of his guitar and our favorite worship songs is priceless.

I was reading my Bible one day and stumbled upon Isaiah 56:1, 2: "This is what the Lord says: 'Maintain justice and do what is right, for my salvation is close at hand and my righteousness will soon be revealed. Blessed is the one who does this—the person who holds it fast, who keeps the Sabbath without desecrating it, and keeps their hands from doing any evil.'"

This verse really spoke to me. God sent Isaiah to speak to Judah at a time when they were worshipping, and sacrificing their children to these gods, and intermarrying with other religions. Yet amid all this perversion, God gives Isaiah a message about the Sabbath, saying in verses 6 and 7, "All who keep the Sabbath without desecrating it and who hold fast to my covenant—these I will bring to my holy mountain and give them joy in my house of prayer. Their burnt offerings and sacrifices will be accepted on my altar; for my house will be called a house of prayer for all nations."

The only reason I am even putting this book together is that Christ has revealed to me through prayer and study how important it is that we take Him at His word. I have realized that we are living in an age where nothing means anything. If you are certain about something, you are considered closed minded. If you believe something is wrong or sinful, even if you cite biblical texts to explain your position, you are deemed a bigot. The world will tell you self-righteously that it is right and God is wrong.

Christians no longer understand the difference between right and wrong because they don't want to offend anyone. Here's the thing: you can love people *and* disagree with their choices. A cruel lie has been spun for love to mean acceptance and disapproval to mean rejection. Tell me Satan's hands aren't filthy in all of this. Tell me this isn't the same serpent that played word games with Eve. His tongue is his prized arsenal, and he is destroying humanity with every lie, twisted word, and web he weaves.

We must know why we believe what we believe. We must be able to explain to others why we believe what we believe. We must know with confidence that God is who He said He is and that He does what He says He will do. I believe we are gearing up for the last leg of this race before Christ returns—there isn't time to mess around.

Elijah should serve as our example for how connected we must be to God in order to be a part of that generation who never tastes death, but lives to see Christ return. Elijah never died, but was met with chariots of fire and taken to heaven. This illustration is symbolic of the generation that will not die and will meet the Son of man as He descends from heaven to take us to Him. Elijah was a man of great faith who believed that God would do what He said. He was fed by ravens during the drought and watched fire fall from heaven on Mount Carmel. He was able to stand in confidence because he knew that when God said He would show up, He would show up.

If you too wish to represent this last generation as Christ returns, you must build your personal relationship with Christ and become like Elijah. You must have faith in your Redeemer and know with conviction that He is who He said He was and will do what He said He would. When Jesus tells us to take heart because He has overcome the world, He has overcome the world! "I have told you these things, so that in me you may have peace. In this world you will have trouble. But take heart! I have overcome the world" (John 16:33).

Ellen White tells about a vision God gave her in 1851 about the church of the last days. She says that many will not understand that in order to be standing when Christ returns, they will need to be filled with the Spirit and reflect the image of Christ. "I also saw that many do not realize what they must be in order to live in the sight of the Lord without a high priest in the sanctuary through the time of trouble. Those who receive the seal of the living God and are protected in the time of trouble must reflect the image of Jesus fully."[6]

The last sentence on that page is: "Let all remember that God is holy and that none but holy beings can ever dwell in His presence."[7] After reading that, I finally understood what it will take to be left standing as the last Christians in that last moment before Christ's return.

White says that the last-day church must teach the news of present truth. "There are many precious truths contained in the Word of God, but it is 'present truth' that the flock needs now. I have seen the danger of the messengers running off from the important points of present truth, to dwell upon subjects that are not calculated to unite the flock and sanctify the soul. Satan will here take every possible advantage to injure the cause."[8]

So what do we focus on? Present truth. We need to spend our efforts uniting the flock and rallying the troops. What exactly is present truth? She continues: "But such subjects as the sanctuary, in connection with the 2300 days, the commandments of God and faith of Jesus, are perfectly calculated to explain the past Advent movement and show what our present position is, establish the faith of the doubting, and give certainty to the glorious future."[9]

Ellen White says that present truth is God's imminent return, the Ten Commandments, and messages of faith. Share your Sabbath in connection with the Ten Commandments, share your knowledge of prophecy in connection with His soon return, and share your testimony to build the faith of others. Share all of this present truth with a people who are thirsty for it. But before you do that, recognize just exactly who you are an ambassador for—God! And our Savior lives.

Response to Critic Number Eight

Claim: Sunday is the Sabbath.

Reply: I'll refer you to this quote published in the *Catholic Press* on August 25, 1900: "Sunday is a Catholic institution, and its claims to observance can be defended only on Catholic principles.... From beginning to end of Scripture there is not a single passage that warrants the transfer of weekly public worship from the last day of the week to the first."[10]

---

[1] James Cardinal Gibbons, *The Faith of Our Fathers*, 16th ed., p. 111.

[2] E. Lonnie Melashenko, *What the Bible Says About . . .* (Nampa, Idaho: Pacific Press Pub. Assn., 2003), p. 45.

[3] *Ibid.*, pp. 45, 46.

[4] Loron Wade, *The Ten Commandments* (Hagerstown, Md.: Review and Herald Pub. Assn., 2006), pp. 51, 52.

[5] E. G. White, *Patriarchs and Prophets*, p. 111.

[6] E. G. White, *Early Writings*, p. 71.

[7] *Ibid.*

[8] *Ibid.*, p. 63.

[9] *Ibid.*

[10] "Rampart Sabbatarianism," *Catholic Press* (Sydney, Australia), Aug. 25, 1900.

Chapter 9

I Don't Know About God, but I Do Believe in Ghosts

**"When I'm asked, 'Are you afraid of the dark?'
my answer is 'No, I'm afraid of what is in the dark.'"**
—Barry Fitzgerald

According to an article by *Christian Post* reporter Audrey Barrick in 2007, one third of Americans believe in ghosts.[1] I have no personal experiences with ghosts, and I've never seen an apparition or heard the voice of a friend who has died. Some people have heard and seen these things, so to them, belief in the supernatural is very much a reality. Hollywood is making billions of dollars on ghost movies and television shows about the supernatural. People have a fascination with paranormal activity. Perhaps we want to believe that our loved ones are not gone, or maybe we want to believe that we, too, won't just cease to exist one day. Whatever the reason, Satan is busy perpetuating the very first lie he ever told humankind: "You will not certainly die" (Genesis 3:4).

I think it is important to discuss what the Bible says about ghosts and life after death. Back in Eden, God told Adam and Eve that the result of sin was death. The very first lie we ever hear Satan utter is that God did not mean exactly what He said. The same serpent in Eden is spinning the same lies today. He is tainting our understanding of Scripture by twisting God's words and playing to our desire to be restored to eternal life.

Satan is whispering, "You shall not surely die; your soul will live on. Your body may die, but there is another life after this one; you'll see." This idea of inherent immortality is a problem because it is not the truth. The Bible is clear that the only life after this one is heaven. If you choose to follow Christ and His teachings and you die before He comes, He will raise you up at the same time as the rest of His people who have died in Him—at His second coming—and you will meet Him in the air. His followers who have not died—the last-generation church—will be changed in the blink of an eye, and all of us will go to heaven together. Satan will be left on earth with his angels to witness the destruction he has caused.

As we look into what the Bible says about death, I will again be drawing from E. Lonnie Melashenko's book *What the Bible Says About . . .* , mainly from chapter 9, which directs us to several Bible verses on death. We will look first at Ecclesiastes 9:5, 6, which tells us that when a person dies, they simply cease to exist and they know nothing: "For the living know that they will die, but the dead know nothing; they have no further reward, and even their name is forgotten. Their love, their hate, and their jealousy have long since vanished; never again will they have a part in anything that happens under the sun."

Psalm 146:3, 4 repeats this idea: "Do not put your trust in princes, in human beings, who cannot save. When their spirit departs, they return to the ground; on that very day their plans come to nothing."

Psalm 115:17 tells us: "It is not the dead who praise the Lord, those who go down to the place of silence."

In Leviticus 20:27 God warns us against consulting those who claim to be able to communicate with the dead. "A man or woman who is a medium or spiritist among you must be put to death. You are to stone them; their blood will be on their own heads."

So what is the problem with believing that you go to heaven right after you die? The problem is that it opens the door for more of Satan's deceptions. It gives Satan a way to enter into your heart. The Bible says that in the last days the deceptions will be powerful. Matthew 24:24 says: "For false messiahs and false prophets will appear and perform great signs and wonders to deceive, if possible, even the elect."

You may not believe something Satan or some high-ranking public figure tells you is true about how to get to heaven or what God is really like, but if your beloved dead brother, or mother, or sister, or father whom you believe to be in heaven appears in ghostlike form to provide you with an urgent message from God, why would you not believe them? Satan and his angels will take all types of forms in order to deceive you. There is no line they will not cross. It is absolutely imperative that you have a rock-solid foundation on what the Bible says on death, so that if Satan tries to deceive you in this way you will know it.

In Luke 23:42, 43 is a text people often use to say that those who are saved go directly to heaven after death. "Then he said, 'Jesus, remember me when you come into your kingdom.' Jesus answered him, 'Truly I tell you, today you will be with me in paradise.' "

This incident is another time when the principle of *sola scriptura* must be used. Jesus tells the thief on the cross that he will surely be with Him in Paradise. He tells him today, meaning "I am going to give you this hope today, that one day we will be together in paradise." We know that Jesus did not go to heaven immediately after His death, because on Sunday, two days after He was crucified, He told Mary that He had not yet ascended to His Father in heaven. "Jesus said, 'Do not hold on to me, for I have not yet ascended to the Father. Go instead to my brothers and tell them, "I am ascending to my Father and your Father, to my God and your God"'" (John 20:17).

This shows us clearly that when Christ spoke to the thief on the cross, He was giving him the assurance on that very day, the day of his repentance, that he would eventually join Him in heaven.

In Acts 2:34 Peter points out that King David, who had been dead for centuries, was not currently in heaven: "For David did not ascend to heaven."

Where is David? He is dead; his body has gone back to the earth, and the breath in his lungs has gone back to God.

Genesis 2:7 says: "Then the Lord God formed a man from the dust of the ground and breathed into his nostrils the breath of life, and the man became a living being." When God created Adam, He formed his human body from the dust of the earth. After He formed his body, He breathed into that body the breath of life, or his spirit. Your spirit is simply the breath of life that God provides to every living being. When we die, the process of life reverses itself in a process called death. Our bodies go back to the dust of the earth from which God first formed them, and our spirit—the breath of life in our lungs—goes back to God.

Melashenko says it this way: "The living soul—or living being—ceases to exist. Nowhere in the Bible is the word 'soul' used to mean a conscious, intelligent entity, capable of existence apart from the body."[2]

So should we be afraid to die? I completely understand the fear. It is scary to enter into something you do not know or fully understand. We know that Jesus compared death to the state of being asleep. Actually, the Bible compares death to sleep more than 50 times. John 11:11-14 is one such moment: "After he had said this, he went on to tell them, 'Our friend Lazarus has fallen asleep; but I am going there to wake him up.' His disciples replied, 'Lord, if he sleeps, he will get better.' Jesus had been speaking of his death, but his disciples thought he meant natural sleep. So then he told them plainly, 'Lazarus is dead.'"

From these Bible texts we know that being dead is like being asleep. Death is not bad for the person who dies; in fact, the Bible often refers to death as mercy. "The righteous perish, and no one takes it to heart; the devout are taken away, and no one understands that the righteous are taken away to be spared from evil" (Isaiah 57:1). I don't think we realize how sad this life is until we see what life is supposed to be.

After believers die, it will seem to them as though they've gone straight to heaven. Those who are asleep in death have no thoughts, and the very next thing they will know is that they are face to face with Jesus at His second coming. They will be reunited with friends and family, and their relationship with God will be fully restored.

I think we should view life as a gift; therefore, we should choose it, want it, and make the most out of it. But we also have to recognize that a natural process of this life is death. Our entire lives—if we want them to be—are in God's hands. Sometimes we cannot know or understand why things unfold the way they do, but we just have to trust that God is good and, therefore, His plans are good, and know that heaven is real, that this life is not the end, and that we will meet again with our saved loved ones when Jesus comes back.

I don't think it is the thought of death so much that scares me, but the thought of the life I'll miss. I guess I have this fear of going before I feel ready. I don't want to miss any of my daughter's ballet recitals. I don't want to go before she gets her first boyfriend or has her first kiss and is feeling girl emotions that I will, hopefully, have all the right answers for. I don't want to miss any of my husband's birthdays or kisses or fiddles on his guitar. I think about what I'll miss and that scares me, but I know that death itself is not to be feared.

I think the beauty of death, though, is that it can give us a greater appreciation for life. Sometimes I get stressed out about bills or school or work and I forget what a gift I am living. In those instances when I take a moment to think about how blessed I am to have people who love me, I remember that nothing else matters. My sole purpose on this earth is to receive love and give love away. I want to make people feel special, and I want to feel special. I want to tell friends about the beautiful Savior I have met, and I want to die knowing that I will see those same friends again in heaven. I want to make sure that I had crucial conversations that matter with everyone within my reach. I desperately want to fulfill the destiny for which He created me. My prayer to God is that He won't allow me to die if He still has work for me to do.

Perhaps the harder situation in which to see anything good is not your own death, but that of someone you love. I can imagine no greater pain. I understand that the thought that the person is not dead but is continuing life in heaven is more pleasing than that they are experiencing nothing. We have to hold tight, though, to the promise of restoration.

My husband was 17 years old when he lost his brother, Tyler, to cancer. Seth's brother was a year and a half older, so they were Irish twins, so to speak, and best friends. That loss has definitely shaped who Seth is. I knew him in sixth grade, while Tyler was alive, and I have known him since Tyler's death. I can say with sincerity that the day Tyler died, Seth died too. He will never be the same person as he was before November 18, 2004. He is forever changed, forever bruised.

They say that time heals all wounds, but I think that may be optimistic. Some wounds are too deep. I do know, however, that my husband cannot wait for the return of Jesus Christ. He cannot wait to see the face of His Savior, and he cannot wait to reunite with his brother. We know for certain that Tyler will be leading our family to heaven. His grave will burst open, and his restored body will dance. What a sweet moment that will be for our family. Just thinking about it brings tears to my eyes because I want it so badly.

No, there are no ghosts, but there is a heaven, and Christ is desperate to take you there. The Bible tells us that heaven will be a place of peace, love, and joy. We will be reunited with our Savior; we will be restored to God's original plan for His creation (Revelation 21; 22:1-5). It will be a paradise without sin. Revelation 7:17 says there will be no more crying or mourning in heaven: "For the Lamb at the center of the throne will be their shepherd; 'he will lead them to springs of living water.' 'And God will wipe away every tear from their eyes.' "

The Bible says that after Christ returns, we will go to heaven. Bible study reveals that before we go to the New Jerusalem on the new earth, which will be after the judgment and before Christ destroys Satan once and for all, we will enter a time period scholars refer to as the "millennium." Melashenko says it this way: "The word *millennium* comes from the Latin words *mille*, meaning 'thousand,' and *annus*, meaning 'year.' Thus *millennium* is a period of one thousand years. The word *millennium* itself does not appear in the Bible, but Revelation 20 describes a thousand-year time period that begins when Jesus returns the second time."[3]

Melashenko points out verses dealing with the millennium such as John 5:28, 29, which says: "Do not be amazed at this, for a time is coming when all who are in their graves will hear his voice and come out—those who have done what is good will rise to live, and those who have done what is evil will rise to be condemned." Every person who has ever died will eventually be brought back to life. Some will be resurrected to meet God in the air, and others will be resurrected only to meet the final judgment scene and eventual condemnation.[4]

Melashenko also points out a passage in 1 Thessalonians in which Paul explains that there are going to be only four groups of people on this earth when Jesus returns: those who are righteous and living, those who are righteous and dead, the living who are wicked, and the dead who were wicked. At the Second Coming the righteous dead will be called from their graves and the righteous living will be caught up in the air. Both of these groups will go to heaven, and the thousand-year period will begin. [5] "For the Lord himself will come down from heaven, with a loud command, with the voice of the archangel and with the trumpet call of God, and the dead in Christ will rise first. After that, we who are still alive and are left will be caught up together with them in the clouds to meet the Lord in the air. And so we will be with the Lord forever" (1 Thessalonians 4:16, 17).

What happens to the living wicked? Remember what Ellen White said in *Early Writings*? "Let all remember that God is holy and that none but holy beings can ever dwell in His presence."[6] They will die and remain dead until the millennium is over.

And what happens to those who were wicked and were already dead? Revelation 20:4, 5 says the wicked dead will remain dead at Jesus' second coming. They will stay in their graves until the judgment scene at the end of the millennium. There is no second chance for them; their lives were lived, and their choices have already been made. They, and the wicked who were living at Jesus' return and were destroyed, will rise only at the judgment scene so that they will understand why they did not receive eternal life.

During the millennium Satan is bound to the earth. Revelation 20:1-3 says: "And I saw an angel coming down out of heaven, having the key to the Abyss and holding in his hand a great chain. He seized the dragon, that ancient serpent, who is the devil, or Satan, and bound him for a thousand years. He threw him into the Abyss, and locked and sealed it over him, to keep him from deceiving the nations anymore until the thousand years were ended. After that, he must be set free for a short time."

Satan is left to see the devastation that sin and rebellion has wrought. Remember that all this was the result of Satan's efforts. First Corinthians 6:2, 3 tells us that the righteous will judge the rest of the world during the millennium: "Or do you not know that the Lord's people will judge the world? And if you are to judge the world, are you not competent to judge trivial cases? Do you not know that we will judge angels? How much more the things of this life!"

In His wisdom and mercy God is allowing the saints to understand why their loved ones who did not make the same choices as they did are not able to receive the gift of heaven. This is the scene that terrifies me. The thought of Jesus explaining to me why my husband or my daughter or my son is not in heaven, but I am, makes my heart ache. Surely I will remember moments of missed opportunity. Conversations I meant to have but didn't. Instances in which I know I could have shown them how sweet it is to have a friend in Jesus.

This is why I tell you that I beg God not to take me until my work is finished. I need to know that I left no rock unturned, that everyone I loved, I fought for. If they deny Christ despite my pleading, then I can rest in my grave peacefully. But if they deny Christ because no one ever showed them an example of authentic Christian discipleship, then the damnation of someone I dearly loved rests also on my head.

If I can implore you to do one thing, it is to be responsible and accountable to those whom you love. Please be a witness and ambassador for Christ to every close friend or family member whom you love dearly. You may not be able to save the world, but you can certainly affect those people who make your world go round. Pray without ceasing, love without giving up, and let your life be an example they can't help noticing.

Revelation 20:3-13 tells us what happens at the end of the millennium. Satan will be set free, and all the wicked will be raised in order to receive their final judgment.

"He [an angel] threw him [the devil] into the Abyss, and locked and sealed it over him, to keep him from deceiving the nations anymore until the thousand years were ended. After that, he must be set free for a short time.

"I saw thrones on which were seated those who had been given authority to judge. And I saw the souls of those who had been beheaded because of their testimony about Jesus and because of the word of God. They had not worshiped the beast or its image and had not received its mark on their foreheads or their hands. They came to life and reigned with Christ a thousand years. (The rest of the dead did not come to life until the thousand years were ended.) This is the first resurrection. Blessed and holy are those who share in the first resurrection. The second death has no power over them, but they will be priests of God and of Christ and will reign with him for a thousand years.

"When the thousand years are over, Satan will be released from his prison and will go out to deceive the nations in the four corners of the earth—Gog and Magog—and to gather them for battle. In number they are like the sand on the seashore. They marched across the breadth of the earth and surrounded the camp of God's people, the city he loves. But fire came down from heaven and devoured them. And the devil, who deceived them, was thrown into the lake of burning sulfur, where the beast and the false prophet had been thrown. They will be tormented day and night for ever and ever.

"Then I saw a great white throne and him who was seated on it. The earth and the heavens fled from his presence, and there was no place for them. And I saw the dead, great and small, standing before the throne, and books were opened. Another book was opened, which is the book of life. The dead were judged according to what they had done as recorded in the books. The sea gave up the dead that were in it, and death and Hades gave up the dead that were in them, and each person was judged according to what they had done."

Philippians 2:10, 11 shows us that even the wicked will acknowledge the goodness and fairness of God: "That at the name of Jesus every knee should bow, in heaven and on earth and under the earth, and every tongue acknowledge that Jesus Christ is Lord, to the glory of God the Father."

This is when the "hellfire" you may have heard of comes about. The wicked, Satan, and the earth in its present sinful state will be burned up by fire from heaven (Revelation 20:9, 10).

And then it is over. The devil is defeated, the earth is made new, and the saints will rejoice forever. Revelation 21:1 says: "Then I saw 'a new heaven and a new earth,' for the first heaven and the first earth had passed away, and there was no longer any sea."

So this is what we understand from the Bible about ghosts, life after death, heaven, hell, and the new earth. Knowledge is power. Go set your world on fire.

Response to Critic Number Nine

Claim: Ghosts are real.

Reply: This references the very first lie the devil told humankind, "You will not certainly die" (Genesis 3:4). The Bible tells us in Ecclesiastes 9:5, "For the living know that they will die; but the dead know nothing, and they have no more reward, for the memory of them is forgotten" (NKJV).

---

[1] www.christianpost.com/news/how-many-americans-believe-in-ghosts-spells-and-superstition-29857.

[2] E. L. Melashenko, *What the Bible Says About . . .* , p. 29.

[3] *Ibid.,* p. 20.

[4] *Ibid.*

[5] *Ibid.*

[6] E. G. White, *Early Writings,* p. 71.

Chapter 10

But I Am a Loser— What Would God Want With Me?

"I decided to get sober when I took a look around the house I was at one day, and saw nothing but losers. My friends, the losers, sitting around staring at the walls, talking about nothing, and repeating the same patterns every day. I thought about where I would be in five years, if I stayed with this crowd, and I saw myself as one of the losers, so I went home and told my mum that I needed to get out of that scene now."

—Jack Osbourne

I had planned to write this last chapter on prayer. I had been doing a bunch of prayer research, and I wanted to talk about the power of prayer. I was going to tell you that 87 percent of Americans believe in prayer, according to a survey by *Newsweek*,[1] and that in a Gallup survey, about three in 10 Americans say they have experienced a "remarkable healing" and credit their own or others' prayers as the cause.[2] However, there have been countless studies done that yielded mixed results. When scientists try to clinically analyze if prayer works, by assigning a set of patients to a set of Christians whom they ask to pray for them, results typically do not show any difference between the prayed-for patients and the not-prayed-for patients. Does that mean that prayer simply doesn't work?

Then I was going to explain how I do not think you can scientifically test prayer. There just seems something so egocentric about that idea. The thought of creation testing the Creator by assigning random tests and cases just doesn't feel right. That seems to go against what prayer even is. Prayer is power when we pray correctly. We should pray out of brokenness and submission, a longing for Christ to be seen, and desperate for a glimpse of His presence. J. I. Packer once wrote about prayer, saying it is "not an attempt to force God's hand, but a humble acknowledgment of helplessness and dependence."[3]

I wanted to tell you that when done correctly, when done out of love and a yearning to be one with God, prayer has so much power. I have seen it, felt it, watched it, and wrapped myself tightly around it. I had gotten about this far when I couldn't ignore any longer God's tugging at my heart. I can cite statistics on prayer, I can explain that prayer is power, but if you don't know God personally, you'll never feel an ounce of it.

I felt God redirecting me, and I asked Him what would hurt your prayers. I shut down my laptop and prayed, asking Him to use me and to guide my words so they could reach you where you need them. I don't know your circumstances or how you came by this book. I don't know your home life or work life or love life. I don't know why you need God or want God or how your relationship with Him is coming along. I do know, though, that God knows you.

Forget the clinical studies and the research. Prayer without a personal relationship with Christ will be of no use to you. Understanding how it works and the right things to say means nothing because when you meet God, He just wants you to talk to Him. He doesn't care if you are using the right words; He just wants to form a connection. He wants you to be open enough to talk and share and then be still for a while to listen.

The biggest thing in my life that has hurt my relationship with Jesus is guilt. I've done so many things I am not proud of. Things I will probably never say aloud. In my past I've embarrassed God, and I've let guilt separate us. I understood that God was real, but I felt that there was no way this real God would want anything to do with me. It took me years to remove the separation I had allowed guilt to cause between God and me. Oh, I prayed, but they were surface-level prayers. I didn't know what to say to Him, and I didn't really want Him close to me. I wanted Him to keep His distance because I guess I thought that as long as He wasn't too close, He would continue loving me.

The thing is, God wants to get close. In fact, He wants to live in you! Regardless of what you've done, or where you've been, or who you currently are, God wants to live in you. He wants to start over. He wants you to know that He sees incredible things in you and has an unbelievable plan for you, and He is just hoping that you will be still and let Him be near you.

There are days I still feel like a loser. I don't mean to make it sound as though I've never missed a night's sleep since I met God. Sometimes I cry at night. Sometimes I bury my head in my pillow and wail so hard the bed shakes. I don't always know what brings on these fits. Maybe it was a word that struck the wrong chord that day, but sometimes it's just me facing reality and realizing that even though no one else knows what I've done or who I've been, I always will.

Sometimes I cry not because of what I have done, but because of what I haven't done. There are so many things I know I should have done, yet didn't do. At the time of inspiration, I'm on fire. I can't wait to get my hands dirty and dive right into whatever project it is I'm developing. Then, somewhere in the midst of the planning and the implementation, my engine goes on empty. I put it aside, fully intending to pick it back up later. But then I lose the initiative.

And then it happens. Reality hits. My bottom lip quivers, and it's all a downward spiral from there. These episodes usually come on when I'm feeling unfulfilled, or when I know there's something God wants me to finish. A book or a project He has placed on my heart that I've pushed so far back on my to-do list that it's forgotten. And then He strips away the layers of my vanity and grabs my attention so tightly that it hurts not to finish the project. But the first step is always the crying.

I miss the days of childhood when crying came naturally, when I cried because it was my first inclination. Now I'm always fighting it back and holding it in so that I can look like an adult. But just as you wouldn't leave a lid on a pot full of boiling water very long, you can't cap your emotions and expect them not to overflow. Eventually something's going to explode, and you'd better hope you have some rags handy to mop up the mess.

With God, it's OK to explode. It's OK to let it all out and go where you don't want to. It's OK to uncap the death of your mom, deal with your own sickness, or face the demons of your guilt. God doesn't just want the perfect you—He wants all of you. Once I understood that with God it was OK just to be myself, I was freed. Even when I cry, I find peace. In all honesty, I rarely feel burdened by my past mistakes anymore. I have felt the calming arms of God wrapped around me in mercy. I know He has seen me and forgives me and loves me anyway. I can breathe.

I watched a YouTube video in which a young guy was talking about this sex education video he had recently seen. It showed a guy about to drink a bottle of water, and then a bunch of people jump out of a van parked next to him, grab the water bottle from him, and pass it around, taking sips, licking the rim, and taking turns putting their dirty hands all over it. Then they hand the water bottle back to the guy, and a caption appears that reads "Who would want to drink from that bottle now?" The point of the video was that if you have too many sexual partners, no one is ever going to want you.

After explaining what happened in the video, the young guy kind of shook his head in disbelief. "You want to know who wants that water bottle?" he said with a hint of a smile. "God does."

I couldn't agree with him more. God does. In spite of what you've done, God still wants you. In fact, He is downright desperate for you to make your move. Satan is filling your head with lies when he tells you that you are not good enough, that you aren't going to amount to anything. God's strength is made perfect through your weakness (2 Corinthians 12:9), so stop separating yourself from Him and thinking you are hiding who you really are. God wants to show you who you're supposed to become.

Sometimes I think about how hard it must be to be God. He loves people who reject Him, tries to hold back judgment in hopes of giving out grace to people who mock Him, and delays His return in mercy to a people who, through word and action, deny that He will ever come at all.

According to the Pew Forum on Religion and Public Life, 79 percent of Christians in the United States believe Jesus is coming back.[4] I find that statistic interesting. Seventy-nine percent of the Christian church in America believes that Christ is returning, but do we really? I'm sure we all would adjust something about our lifestyles if we truly believed that next month, or even next year, we would see the Son of Man descending from the heavens ready to take His followers home. If God was coming tomorrow, what would you be doing today?

I think most Christians believe in the Second Coming in theory, but do our current lives have any resemblance to this belief? Of course, it doesn't really matter if Christ doesn't come back tomorrow, next week, next month, or in the next 10 years. The truth is, none of us are promised another moment. Even if Christ didn't return for 100 years, we could still die tomorrow, which means the very next thing we might see is the return of our Lord. Every day we wake up could be the day we die, so we need to live every day prepared to stand before Jesus.

First Thessalonians 5:3 says: "While people are saying, 'Peace and safety,' destruction will come on them suddenly, as labor pains on a pregnant woman, and they will not escape." While the world is working on fixing its economy, while we are in the midst of an election or new presidency, when everyone is saying things are really starting to look up, disaster and calamity will happen suddenly. The time of trouble will begin like labor pains. I have given birth, so let me break down for you what that means.

One minute you feel fine, and the next minute you feel the first pains of labor. It starts off slow, and you think, *Oh, this isn't so bad.* As time progresses the pains get more intense and you think, *Surely this is the worst of it.* Then, before you know it, there is pain so blinding and catastrophic that you can't move or talk or be comforted. All you can do is struggle to breathe and scream. God's description here of what the end of time will be like may be lost on some, but certainly not on any woman who has gone through labor. This analogy is striking.

But here is the beauty: after the pain is over and the tears have stopped, you have a child, a tiny, perfect, sweet human being. Never mind that just moments ago you would have contemplated death before continuing on in this agony; now you'd fight to the death before you would let anything separate you from this child. And that is what heaven will be like after we survive the time of trouble, a time in earth's history so depleting that Jesus warns us in Matthew 24:22, "If those days had not been cut short, no one would survive, but for the sake of the elect those days will be shortened." He knew we would be afraid, so He promised, "I am with you always, to the very end of the age" (Matthew 28:20). After we survive this harrowing ordeal, we will receive the kingdom of heaven, a perfect, sweet place where sin will never separate us from God again.

In the meantime, take some time every day and really try to connect with God through prayer. Let it all out. Press your face to the floor, let go of who you've been, and start today developing a real, personal relationship with Jesus Christ—don't put it off. The truth is, at the end of it all it won't matter how much you know God exists or how academically you can defend Him in a debate. All that will matter is how connected you were to Him in your personal and daily life.

Jesus' disciples often did a lot of dumb stuff. They said the wrong things, missed the point, and sometimes appeared completely incapable of delivering God's message to the entire world. There have been times while I am reading that I have to pause and say, "Really, God? This is the person You chose?"

Again and again Jesus is forced to correct their misinterpretations of what He is saying, and these are the people who are with Him constantly! Let's dive into the book of Mark. Trust me, it won't take us long to find these misfits, these losers, making huge mistakes.

Mark 9:38-41 begins with John saying, "We saw a man driving out demons in your name and we told him to stop, because he was not one of us!" Now, that is coming from John. Jesus knows John and loves John dearly. This is the same John who sat on the island of Patmos penning the book of Revelation. While Jesus is hanging on the cross, He turns and looks at His mother, then turns to John and says that this is your mother. Mother,

John is now your son. Jesus knows and loves John and John knows and loves Jesus, and yet here we see John get it wrong.

We turn to Mark 10:13-16, and again we see the disciples messing up. "People were bringing little children to Jesus for him to place his hands on them, but the disciples rebuked them. When Jesus saw this, he was indignant. He said to them, 'Let the little children come to me, and do not hinder them, for the kingdom of God belongs to such as these. Truly I tell you, anyone who will not receive the kingdom of God like a little child will never enter it.' And he took the children in his arms, placed his hands on them and blessed them." How embarrassing? These are Jesus' best friends! These are His men, the people whom He spends all His time with, and yet in front of everyone He rebukes them. He even goes as far as to say that unless they become like one of these, there is no place for them in His kingdom.

Next we find ourselves in Mark 14:32-42, and Jesus is in the Garden of Gethsemane:

"They went to a place called Gethsemane, and Jesus said to his disciples, 'Sit here while I pray.' He took Peter, James and John along with him, and he began to be deeply distressed and troubled. 'My soul is overwhelmed with sorrow to the point of death,' he said to them. 'Stay here and keep watch.'

"Going a little farther, he fell to the ground and prayed that if possible the hour might pass from him. 'Abba, Father,' he said, 'everything is possible for you. Take this cup from me. Yet not what I will, but what you will.'

"Then he returned to his disciples and found them sleeping. 'Simon,' he said to Peter, 'are you asleep? Couldn't you keep watch for one hour? Watch and pray so that you will not fall into temptation. The spirit is willing, but the flesh is weak.'

"Once more he went away and prayed the same thing. When he came back, he again found them sleeping, because their eyes were heavy. They did not know what to say to him.

"Returning the third time, he said to them, 'Are you still sleeping and resting? Enough! The hour has come. Look, the Son of Man is delivered into the hands of sinners. Rise! Let us go! Here comes my betrayer!'"

Jesus, the God of the heaven and earth, is asking for the help of these sinners at the hour in which He needs it most! He is telling them, "Hey, guys, I'm weak here, I don't know if I can do this." He is sweating blood. His soul is in such agony, and all He asks is for them to do two things: keep watch and pray. Three times He asks them, and three times they fail Him.

Last, at the close of Mark we find ourselves in Mark 16:10-15:

"She went and told those who had been with him and who were mourning and weeping. When they heard that Jesus was alive and that she had seen him, they did not believe it. Afterward Jesus appeared in a different form to two of them while they were walking in the country. These returned and reported it to the rest; but they did not believe them, either. Later Jesus appeared to the Eleven as they were eating; he rebuked them for their lack of faith and their stubborn refusal to believe those who had seen him after he had risen. He said to them, 'Go into all the world and preach the gospel to all creation.'"

Jesus has told them again and again, "You remember the sacrifice Isaiah and Jeremiah prophesied about? You remember the Lord they talked about? I am that Lord and I am that Lamb. I will be crucified, they are going to kill Me, they are going to beat Me, they are going to ruin My physical body, but they will not take My soul. I will be slain, but I will rise again in three days' time, and you will see Me alive in all My father's glory!"

Again and again He tells them this. And yet when in John 20:17 He tells Mary Magdalene (another huge sinner and loser), after she sees Him when He is raised, to go and tell the others what she has seen, and so she runs and she is excited and she finds two disciples and she tells them, "You won't believe it! He is alive! I have seen Him! He spoke to me! He told us He was going to rise! Hd told us He was the lamb that takes away the sins of the world!" they don't believe her. Then two of the disciples leave and start walking, and the next thing they know they find themselves face to face with Jesus, and once they see Him for themselves they believe it is true and they rush off to tell the others and when they get there, none of them believe them. And so Jesus shows up, and He rebukes them once more.

Surely, Lord, You could have found 12 better men then these! What I love about this story, though, is how terrible these guys are and yet how it ends. In the last verse, verse 15, Jesus tells them, "Go into all the world and preach the gospel to all creation." Even after they disappoint Him, even after they don't get it, even after they fail Him time and time again. *Jesus still sees them fit for His mission! He uses them anyway! Hallelujah!*

Here's the secret: the disciples are just like us! They didn't get it, they made mistakes, but guess what, every morning and every evening, whose feet were they beside? Jesus'! I'm telling you, I promise you, get up every morning and go to bed every evening beside the feet of Jesus, and it won't matter if you don't get it, it won't matter if you aren't sure where you are going. Spend your time building a personal daily relationship with Christ, and He will meet you where you are at. He's going to keep working with you and molding you as long as you cling to those feet.

They certainly were not perfect people, but they did do one thing exceptionally well: they began and finished every single day hanging out with Jesus. That is the model and example I try to apply to my own life.

This entire book would be a waste if I didn't stop and ask you to make sure that you are taking time to connect with Jesus daily. Please, if you get only one thing from everything I have said in these 10 chapters, let it be this: Jesus is coming soon, and there is nothing more important in this world than your personal, saving relationship with Him—a relationship He wants so badly that He died to make it possible. Cling to the feet of Jesus, and it won't matter that you are a loser. Regardless of who you are and what you've done, He will find a place to use you. Trust me. So now: "*Go into all the world and preach the gospel to all creation.*"

Response to Critic Number Ten

Claim: But I am a loser—what would God want with me?

Reply: "God wants you to get where God wants you to go more than you want to get where God wants you to go."—Mark Batterson.[5]

---

[1] www.thedailybeast.com/newsweek/1997/03/30/is-god-listening.html.

[2] www.gallup.com/poll/6094/religion-may-body-good.aspx.

[3] J. I. Packer, *Evangelism and the Sovereignty of God* (Downer's Grove, Ill.: InterVarsity Press, 1961), p. 11.

[4] www.pewforum.org/Christians-Views-on-the-Return-of-Christ.aspx.

[5] Mark Batterson, *In a Pit With a Lion on a Snowy Day* (Colorado Springs, Colo.: Multnomah Books, 2008).